Revisiting Public-Private Partnerships in the Power Sector

A WORLD BANK STUDY

Revisiting Public-Private Partnerships in the Power Sector

Maria Vagliasindi

THE WORLD BANK
Washington, D.C.

Contents

Boxes

Figures

Tables

Acknowledgments

The report was developed by a team led by Maria Vagliasindi, Lead Economist, Energy Anchor including Ada Karina Izaguirre, Infrastructure Specialist, FEU, Claudia Hitaj and Sebastian Lopez Azumendi, STC, Energy Anchor, with input from Jie Li, Young Professional, South Asia Enviroment Unit, Evgenia Shumilkina, ETC, Energy Anchor, Jens Wirth and Xiaolu Yu, both JPA, Energy Anchor. Excellent editorial support provided by Laura Wallace. ESMAP financial support and partnership are gratefully acknowledged. Michael Pollitt, jointly with Haney, prepared a background paper on New Models of Public Ownership in Energy. Mercados collected data and prepared a background report on selected countries.

The Report would not have been possible without the invaluable advice, comments, and suggestions of the Expert Advisory, including Emmanuelle Auriol, Professor of Economics, University of Toulouse, France, John Besant-Jones, Lead Energy Adviser, World Bank, Pasquale Cirillo, Lecturer and Fellow in Econometrics and Risk Analysis, Institute of Mathematical Statistics, University of Bern, Switzerland, Istvan Dobozi, Lead Energy Economist, ESMAP, Antonio Estache, Jose Luis Guasch, Paul Grout, Professor of Political Economy, Department of Economics & Centre for Market and Public Organisation, University of Bristol & OFGEM Advisor, UK and Clive Harris, and Jaime Millan, former Principal Energy Economist, Infrastructure and Financial Markets, Sustainable Development Department, IADB. The main results of the Report and the individual case studies have been presented to a number of internal and external learning events, including Energy Week 2011 which was held in March 14–16 and a half a day workshop which was held on June 9, 2011.

Overview Chapter

Revisiting Policy Options on Public-Private Partnerships in the Power Sector

Overview

As the world demand for energy continues to grow, a big question is where will all the energy come from and what will the price tag be. The International Energy Agency (IEA) estimates that globally US$38 trillion must be invested in energy supply infrastructure from 2011 to 2035—with US$17 trillion going just to the power sector. On top of that, enormous sums will be needed in the power sector to handle additional investment needs stemming from the green growth agenda and related policies. Already, in 2008, for the first time, renewable energy (including large hydro) attracted more power sector investment globally than fossil-fuel based technologies (UNEP 2011). By 2035, renewable sources of energy are expected to triple (IEA 2010).

This growth in renewables is being driven by an alignment of global factors:

First, demand for energy from emerging economies has risen sharply. China alone increased its oil consumption by 840,000 barrels a day between 2005 and 2007. Over the next 25 years, 90 percent of the projected growth in global energy demand will come from developing countries, with China, India, Indonesia, and Brazil leading the pack.

Second, competition for energy resources has increased. The higher demand for energy and faster use of natural resources is creating greater competition for limited resources—which sometimes plays out in volatile demand and related price fluctuations.

Third, oil and gas prices have been rising. Whereas historical oil price shocks were primarily caused by physical disruptions of supply, the price run-up of 2007/08 was caused by strong demand confronting stagnating world production. More recently, the uprisings in the Middle East in part helped push the world oil crude price above US$120 in April 2011, although this was still below the July 2008 record of US$145 a barrel. In real terms, these prices are comparable to those that caused the 1973 and 1979 energy crises. But if the oil price rises high enough, the use of alternative clean fuels could help control carbon emissions from fossil fuel use.

Fourth, political concerns about fossil fuel energy security have re-emerged in many countries. Take the case of the European Union (EU). The Ukrainian gas supply crises of 2006 and 2009 resulted in the EU receiving lower supplies of Russian gas, owing to a dispute between Ukraine and the Russian Federation. This development has heightened concerns about gas security in the EU and reduced politicians' willingness to allow the power sector to become more dependent on combined cycle gas turbine power plants (Noel 2009).

Fifth, the Kyoto Protocol's implementation in early 2005, along with greater political interest in climate change has refocused the energy debate. The green growth agenda is now a topic of discussion at the highest political levels, with politicians debating measures to control emissions and switch to a low-carbon growth path.

With such enormous sums needed, public-private partnerships (PPPs) could play a big role. But the financial crisis has raised worries about funding, and much is still not known about how best to attract PPPs. This report reviews the evidence to date with sectoral reforms and considers different approaches in varying circumstances to help outline the potential role of the private and public sector in (1) strengthening the corporate governance of private and public utilities; (2) helping governments to establish legal, regulatory, contractual, and fiscal frameworks; and (3) improved market governance to attract private investment.

Chapter 1 reviews the impact of the recent financial crisis on PPP investment compared with what happened in earlier financial crises. It also looks out the latest projections for additional power sector investment needed because of climate change and the possible sources of financing. Chapter 2 examines how PPP investment in the power sector has fared. It also gives the results of an econometric study that explores which types of incentives and variables matter most to PPPs when they are weighing entering the power sector, especially in renewables, and what influences the ongoing level of investment. The idea is to provide a powerful benchmarking tool at the sector and country levels against which governments and policy makers can evaluate progress on this issue. Chapter 3 examines four case studies—in China, Brazil, Peru, and Mexico—to identify, disseminate, and promote best practices on alternative ways to attract PPPs.

The key messages are:

- While many private electricity projects have been delayed and financing costs have increased, the impact of the global financial crisis was less severe than that of previous crises that originated in developing countries
- This resilience stems from developing countries' need to expand generation capacity, electricity sector reforms and better regulatory frameworks, packages to attract independent power producers, and short-term solutions (such as rental power plants)

- Although the crisis brought both short-term relief—lower electricity demand to take the pressure off supply shortages—it also brought longer term problems—higher financing costs for infrastructure
- The sharply reduced appetite of commercial banks for long-term financing in many countries makes international financing institutions especially valuable for private projects
- When weighing whether to enter the power sector, PPPs weigh sectoral governance (feed-in tariffs and electricity regulation), economy-wide governance (control of corruption and degree of democracy), short-run economic drivers (population and income), and long-run climate change (PPP investment in transmission and renewables, the oil price, and legal commitments, such as the Kyoto Protocol, and green policies).

Why Attracting PPPs Matters

What exactly are PPPs and why do they matter so much in the power sector? Ever since a first wave of reform in the 1970s and 1980s, policy makers, donors, and international financial institutions (IFIs) have attempted to improve performance while maintaining public ownership. But these attempts to reform state-owned enterprises (SOEs) largely failed, except for a few difficult-to-sustain exceptions. For instance, performance-based contracts were introduced, as were a number of managerial and policy reforms aimed at increasing the autonomy and accountability of managers, reforming the nature and functions of SOE boards of directors, introducing and reinforcing financial and managerial information systems, and pursuing a range of other mechanisms short of ownership change. Typically, SOE reforms were not implemented or failed to produce the desired results. Even when successes were recorded, they could not be sustained over time.

For that reason, in the 1990s, there was a big push for privatization and the use of PPPs (see box O.1)(see table O.1). **By 2004, PPPs already represented the lion's share in electricity generation and distribution, particularly in middle-income countries.**

However, even after 20 or more years of electricity market reforms, there is still an unfinished agenda. As noted in Pollitt's (2009) review of progress with electricity market reforms in the European Union (EU), it is difficult to find

Table O.1 PPPs Play a Major Role in Developing Country Power Sectors
extent of private sector participation in developing countries as of 2004

Existence of private capital	Low income	Lower middle income	Upper middle income
Electricity generation	41% (59)	48% (42)	58% (33)
Electricity distribution	29% (62)	37% (43)	48% (33)

Source: Estache and Goicoechea 2005.
Note: The entries refer to the shares of sample of countries with some form of private capital (percent of total sample size for each country is given in parenthesis).

Box O.1

A Snapshot of PPPs

A PPP takes the form of a contract between a private sector entity and the government that calls for the private sponsor to deliver a desired service and assume the associated risks in exchange for the right to earn an adequate return. The government may be currently providing that service, or it may be a new service that would benefit the country and economy. Risk allocation is at the heart of how PPPs are structured. In other words, the public sector passes on a portion of the risk of service delivery to the private sector.

The nature of the partnership between the private and the public sector can range from fairly simple contractual arrangements to supply a specific service, to complex arrangements to design, construct, operate, maintain, finance, and provide services. The figure below illustrates the broad spectrum of private sector participation in service delivery. As more equity and control is transferred to the private sector, so too are the risks, commercial and noncommercial. PPPs, in which the private sector can provide significant amounts of financing for the project, may provide relief to government budgets, as well as significant transfers of skills and know-how. With these savings, the government could invest in projects that are less amenable to PPPs.

The majority of new investment in electricity generation has been through build-operate-transfer contracts, sometimes combined with leases for existing plants. The absence of liberalized wholesale power markets means that investors rely on long-term agreements with (usually) state-controlled or guaranteed purchasers. Under these conditions, it is natural to link the purchase agreement to the license to operate the power plant. From a regulatory point of view, however, the downside of long-term power purchase agreements is that they can impede subsequent liberalization and the introduction of competition.

Management and outsourcing contracts are operating contracts without any investment obligations. In the early phase of privatization, most countries were focused on divesting assets, but in recent years, these contracts have become more common as countries have found it harder to attract private operators if the government is hesitant to impose cost-reflective tariffs or cede control of the basic network infrastructure.

Figure BO.1 PPPs Structure Cross a Wide Spectrum

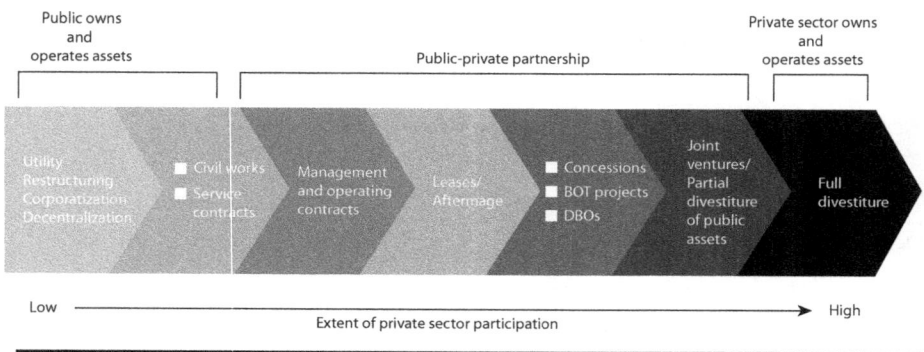

Public owns and operates assets — Public-private partnership — Private sector owns and operates assets

Utility Restructuring Corporatization Decentralization | Civil works / Service contracts | Management and operating contracts | Leases/ Affermage | Concessions / BOT projects / DBOs | Joint ventures/ Partial divestiture of public assets | Full divestiture

Low ———————————— Extent of private sector participation ———————————— High

conclusive evidence of the consistently beneficial effects of the reforms actually implemented in many countries. A more recent review revisiting policy options for unbundling for developing countries (Vagliasindi and Besant Jones, 2012) shows a current distribution of power markets around intermediate structures between full integration and full unbundling that suggests there has not been a linear path to reform in practice. Instead, many developing countries may retain intermediate structures for foreseeable future. For now, PPPs, and in some cases public ownership, remain a significant way in which governments can attempt to insure against and potentially prevent undesirable outcomes of embracing the classic paradigm of private sector participation as a fit to all strategy.

How PPPs Weathered the Financial Crisis

While many private electricity projects have been delayed and financing costs have increased, the impact of the global financial crisis—with 15 large projects implemented in 2009—was less severe than that of previous crises that originated in developing countries. Investment commitments to PPP electricity projects in developing countries reached US$46.5 billion in 2007, about double that of the previous year, and remained around the same level in 2008. Such a level represents an increase of over 150 percent from the level in 2004, and brings investment just 17 percent below the peak level reached in 1997. However, this recovery was highly selective. Three countries—Brazil, India, and the Russia—accounted for most of the growth in 2007–09 (figure O.1).

This resilience stems from developing countries' need to expand generation capacity, electricity sector reforms and better regulatory frameworks, packages to attract independent power producers, and short-term solutions (such as rental power plants). The crisis brought short-term relief—lower electricity demand to take the pressure off supply shortages. However, it also brought longer-term problems in the form of higher financing costs for infrastructure.

Compounding matters is that the new green growth agenda imposes significant new investment requirements on the power sector. Private sector investment is critically needed, but it is unlikely to provide the daunting scale of financing required in the coming decades. Continuous technological improvements (combined with reasonably benign fossil fuel prices) ensured significant real unit cost reductions in power costs (and even larger reductions in the costs of energy services) between 1900 and 2000. However, since then, climate policy (with the objective of reducing carbon dioxide and equivalent greenhouse gases (GHG)) and sister policies aimed at promoting the percentage of electricity generated by renewables (and to reduce demand in high demand countries) have begun to significantly drive costs in many power sectors.

While this has mainly affected Organisation for Economic Co-operation and Development (OECD) countries (particularly within Europe), it has implications for developing countries many of whom have adopted renewable policies. China now is the largest investor in renewable energy, with the United States

Figure O.1 The Recovery Has Mainly Benefited Three Countries

investment commitments to electricity PPP projects in developing countries

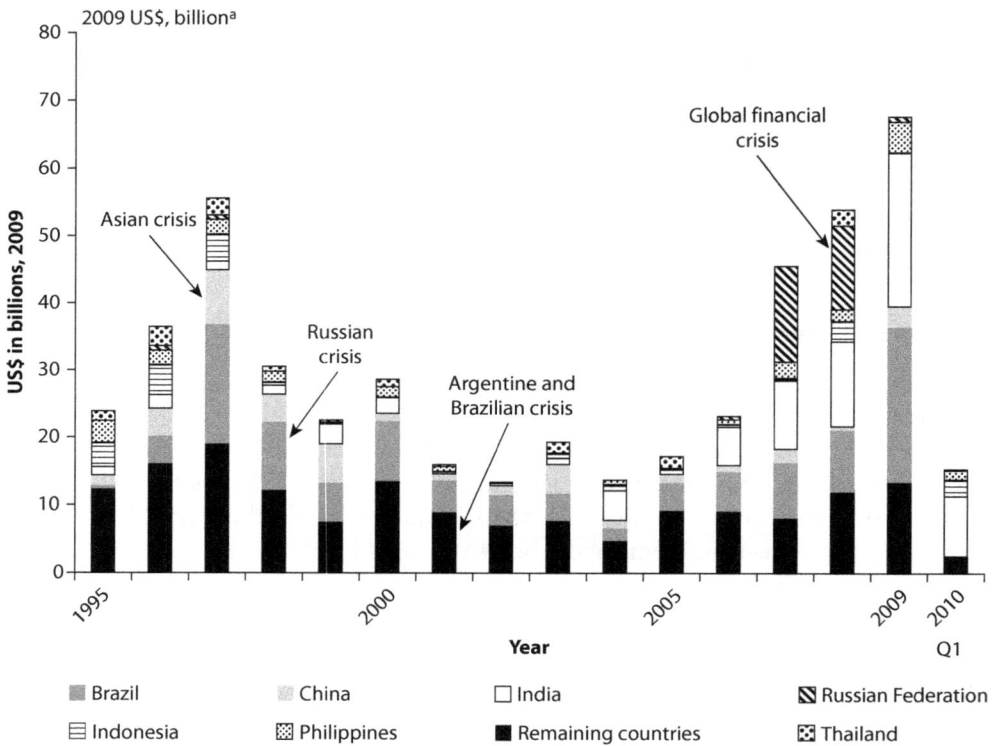

Sources: World Bank and PPIAF, PPI Project Database.
Note: Includes additional investments in projects that reached financial or contractual closure in 1990–2009.
a. Adjusted by US CPI.

far behind (figure O.2), and it has 24+ gigawatts (GW) of wind capacity—the third highest in the world—and this capacity is growing rapidly.

The industrial countries' greater focus on greening growth has indirectly created learning benefits for other countries in renewables and funding for projects via the Clean Development Mechanism of the UN Framework Convention on Climate Change (UNFCCC)—which allows for creating tradable carbon credits from investments in renewable projects in the developing world. But the downside may be a slowing of technical progress and investment in conventional generation technologies.

The policy targets at the individual country level are ambitious and create significant investment requirements for the power sector. Such investments in low carbon generation (such as nuclear) and renewables exposes investors to substantial government policy change risks, especially given that the payback periods for many of these investments are long (15–30 years). PPPs and public ownership may be a way to ensure that the large scale investment requirements

Figure O.2 China Leading the Way in Investing in Renewable Energy

new financial investment in renewable energy, 2011, US$ billion

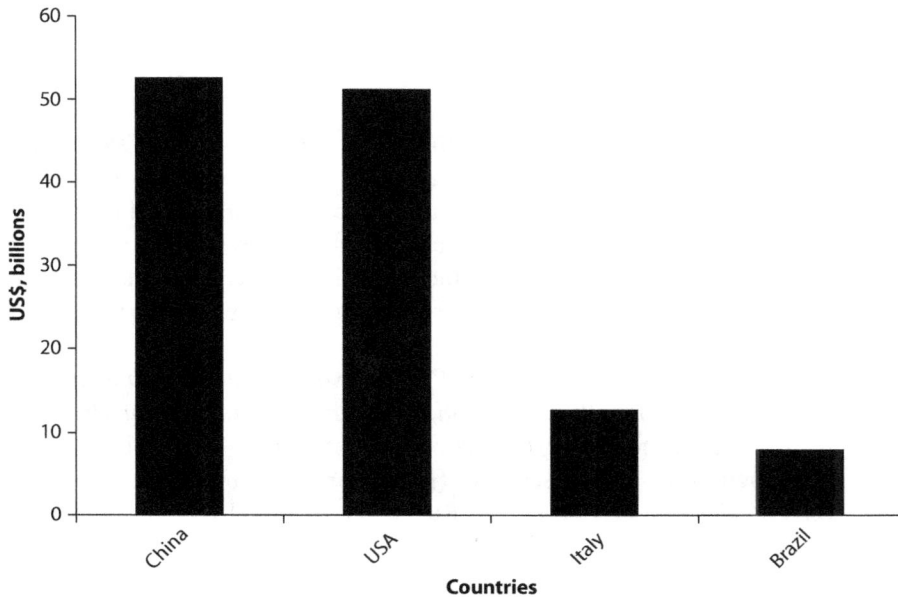

Source: Bloomberg New Energy Finance.

of the power sector are met. Moreover, post-financial crisis, the sharply reduced appetite of commercial banks for long-term financing in many countries makes international financing institutions especially valuable for private projects.

One result of the changed market environment is the increased uncertainty on whether investment will be able to catch up with future demand for power and climate change targets. According to the results of a global survey carried out in 2009 by Price Waterhouse Coopers (2009), two-thirds of about 70 senior power utility executives report that a shortage of capital is having a major impact on their activities. Senior executives in our survey are worried about the high costs also driven by greater uncertainty associated with projects. Two-thirds also refer to problems in securing finance as a medium or high barrier to project development.

Surveyed power utilities emphasize the importance of greater clarity of climate change policy but express concern that the economic recession is undermining the chances of an effective response to climate change. Nearly 60 percent feel that their renewable energy investment programs are being affected by the lack of clarity from governments on renewable energy targets and financial support for renewable energy. The importance of greater certainty on both targets and economic mechanisms to support renewable energy is highlighted by the fact that only 28 percent of respondents believe that unsubsidized renewable power can compete commercially against fossil fuel generation.

Asked if the economic recession would slow down responses to climate change, 79 percent felt it would, with two thirds of the 79 percent saying it would have a high or very high slowdown impact.

Best Ways to Attract PPPs

Which types of energy are PPPs investing in? Of the total PPP investment in electricity generation, fossil fuels account for the lion's share—about 75 percent (figure O.3). Coal accounts for 35 percent, natural gas 24 percent, and fuel oil 15 percent. Total investment in renewables represents a mere 4 percent, if hydropower, at 22 percent, is excluded. Within that group, wind and geothermal technologies have almost an equal share of about 40 percent, with waste limited to 20 percent.

Although the current share of PPP investment in renewables among developing countries is still quite small, the data show a dramatic rise in this type of investment—following the adoption of the Kyoto Protocol in 1997 and the introduction of support schemes (particularly feed-in tariffs) in Europe in the early 1990s. The East Asian and Russian crises in 1997/98, as well as the Latin American crisis in 2001, hurt PPP investments in renewables, but recent short-run shocks have taken less of a toll.

Among the fossil fuels, there is some evidence of switching of PPP investment from oil and coal to natural gas. Indeed, natural gas is the only fossil fuel that has substantially increased its share of PPP investment from about 10 percent in the early 1990s to above 50 percent in 2002, then decreasing to below 40 percent in 2008—although in dollar terms, 2008 was a peak, with investment reaching above US$12 billion. There is also some evidence of switching of PPP investment from fossil fuels to hydro and renewables.

Figure O.3 PPP Investment in Renewables is Still Small and Mostly in Wind and Geothermal

a. Coal, Oil, Nature Gas, Hydro, and Renewables   **b. Geothermal, Waste, Wind, and Solar**

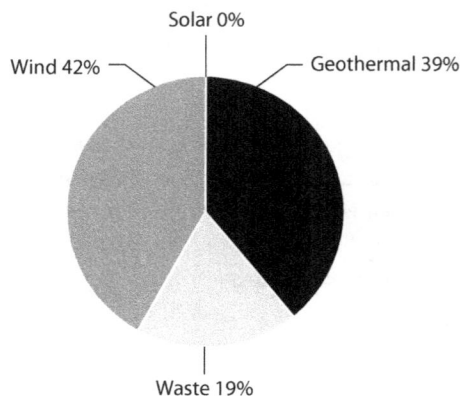

a. Coal, Oil, Nature Gas, Hydro, and Renewables:
Renewables 4%, Hydro 22%, Coal 35%, Natural gas 24%, Oil 15%

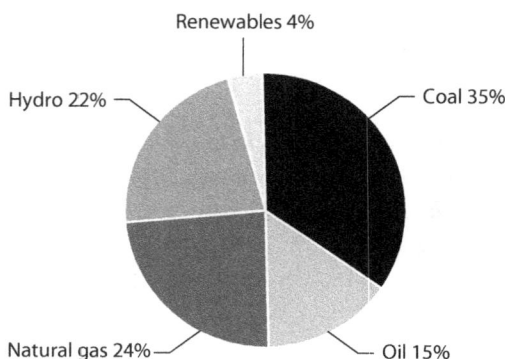

b. Geothermal, Waste, Wind, and Solar:
Solar 0%, Wind 42%, Geothermal 39%, Waste 19%

Source: World Bank/PPIAF PPI Database.

Given this strong need to attract PPP investment in the power sector, our study examined which types of incentives matter most, not just for entry but for the level of investment. We found that for entry all of the variables—sectoral and economy-wide governance, short-term economic drivers, and long-run climate change—are critical but the governance variables are less critical than the other ones for the level of investment (see tables O.2 and O.3).

The highlights are:

- Control for corruption and degree of political competition primarily affect investors' decisions to enter the various power sector markets, not the subsequent level of investment—indicating that investors seem to be adequately protected against risks
- Support mechanisms, like feed-in tariffs, are crucial for attracting investors in renewable generation, but they do not succeed in displacing fossil fuel investment and they could play a bigger role in affecting the level of investment in renewables.
- The implementation of the Kyoto Protocol combined with higher fuel prices is important in attracting PPPs in renewables, underscoring the value of legal commitments.
- Market size (as measured by population) matters more than the "affordability" level of consumers (as measured by income) for attracting PPPs in the power sector. Both variables play a key role in affecting the level of investments.

Table O.2 Before Entering the Power Market, PPPs Weigh Governance, Economic Fundamentals, and Climate Change

key determinants of introduction of PPP investment in power sector

	GEN	REN	T&D	T	D
Sectoral governance variables					
Introduction of feed-in tariffs	$+^{**}$	$+^{**}$	—	—	—
Electricity regulation	—	—	$+^{***}$	$+^{**}$	$+^{*}$
Economy-wide governance variables					
Control of corruption	$+^{***}$	$+^{**}$	—	—	—
Degree of democracy	$+^{**}$	$+^{*}$	—	$+^{**}$	$+^{**}$
Macroeconomic control					
GDP	$+^{***}$	—	$+^{***}$	$+^{***}$	$+^{***}$
Population	$+^{***}$	$+^{***}$	$+^{***}$	$+^{***}$	$+^{***}$
Long-run climate change					
PPP Investment in transmission	$+^{**}$	$++^{**}$	—	—	—
PPP Investment in renewables	—	—	$+^{***}$	$+^{***}$	$+^{***}$
Price of oil	$-^{**}$	—	—	—	—
Price of oil*Kyoto protocol	$+^{**}$	$+^{*}$	—	—	—

Source: World Bank data.
Note: *, **, *** indicate significance of the coefficient, respectively, at 10 percent, 5 percent, and 1 percent confidence level.
— = variables not included in the regression.

Table O.3 Governance Does Not Affect the *Level* of PPP Investment, which Is Largely Driven by Economic Fundamentals and Climate Change

key determinants of the level of PPP investments

	GEN	REN	FF	T&D
Sectoral governance variables				
Introduction of feed-in tariffs	—	+*	—	—
Regulation	—	—	—	—
Economy wide governance variables				
Control of corruption	—	—	—	—
Degree of democracy	—	—	—	—
Long run economic fundamentals				
GDP	+***	+***	+***	+***
Population	+**	+**	+***	+*
Long-run environmental sustainability factors				
PPP Investment in transmission	—	+***	—	—
PPP Investment in renewables	—	—	—	+***
Price of oil	—	+*	—	—
Price of oil*Kyoto protocol	—	+***	—	—

Note: *, **, *** indicate significance of the coefficient, respectively, at 10 percent, 5 percent, and 1 percent confidence level.
— = variables not included in the regression.

Best Practices in Four Developing Countries

The final part of our study zeroed in on the experience of four countries in two regions—China, Brazil, Peru, and Mexico—with using various types of support mechanisms. It also examined the role that PPPs should play in efficiently expanding a transmission network system with natural monopoly characteristics and thus subject to public regulation. The countries chosen represented a wide range of schemes aimed at promoting renewable energies, different ownership (fully private or public or a mix) and market structures, and different levels of renewable energy penetration (table O.4).

The case study evidence suggests that:

There is a significant trade-off between effectiveness and efficiency of alternative instruments for deploying renewables. Feed-in tariffs tended to be quite effective but to be set on the high side, reducing incentives to cut costs and posing significant strains on already stripped national budgets. Competitive auctions, on the other hand have tended to be efficient but initially low and not always the most effective instrument.

Countries can scale up renewables following different paths. For Brazil, the move from feed-in tariffs to auctions enabled it to both reduce costs and deploy additional capacity. Peru followed in Brazil's path, opting for auctions instead of introducing feed-in tariffs. On the other hand, China's move from competitive tenders to feed-in tariffs allowed for discovery effects to determine the right level of prices to attract private investment in renewables.

Table O.4 Case Study Taxonomy

	Ownership	Market structure	Incentives/mechanisms to promote renewable energies	Renewable energy penetration
China	Mainly state-owned.	Organizational unbundling	Mainly feed-in tariffs	17% of total electricity installed capacity (15.7% of hydro, 0.7% of wind, and 0.6% of biomass) 2011 data
Mexico	Mainly state-owned.	Vertically integrated structure	Open Season mechanism to connect renewable energy to the transmission network. The state utility builds the infrastructure based on RE developers' interest. RE producers pay for the infrastructure	16.6% of total electricity production (16.5% of hydro, 0.1% of wind) 2008 data.
Brazil	Mixed public and private owned (30% in the distribution sector, 90% in the generation sector, and almost 100% in the transmission segment).	Single buyer model through a centralized purchasing entity	Move from feed-in tariffs (ProInfra) to auctions.	82% of total electricity production (77% of hydro, 5% of biomass) 2010 data.
Peru	70% of total electricity capacity is generated by private companies. In the transmission segment, all companies are private. In the distribution sector the State and the private sector have similar levels of participation.	Ownership unbundling	Use of auctions as a way of incentivizing the use of renewable energy. So far, 2 auctions have taken place.	60% of total electricity production (almost all renewable energy in Peru comes from hydro sources; only a small percentage, 0.7 MW, comes from wind). 2009 data.

Source: World Bank data.

Private investors require technical and regulatory certainty about the availability of renewable-ready transmission resources if they are to finance investments. The traditional reactive model of transmission regulation—developing transmission on a first-come, first-served basis—is not conducive for renewables, as it introduces extensive regulatory and technical uncertainty about whether adequate transmission will be available once the resource is generated, and transmission distances for renewables can be large. The case of China is quite telling in that the sharp increase in renewables (particularly wind) (figure O.4) posed challenges to the stability of the transmission system. In contrast, Mexico used an open season approach, with new transmission investment decided through an agreement between the Federal Electricity Commission and private investors, which facilitated better regulatory and technical certainty.

Figure O.4 China's Installed Wind Power Capacity Has Skyrocketed

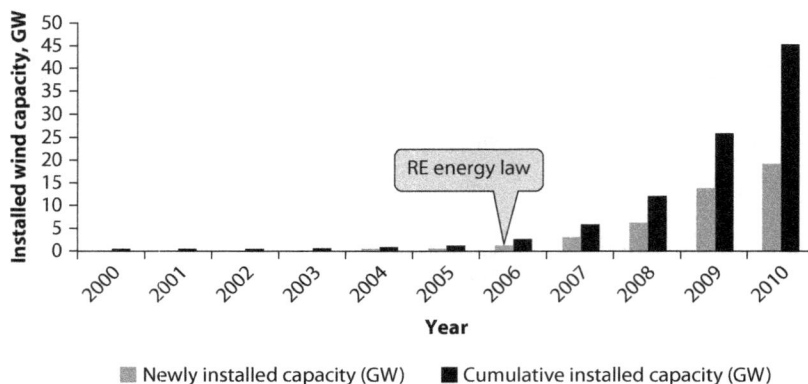

Sources: Junfeng *et al.* 2010; REN21 2011.

References

Estache, A., and A. Goicoechea. 2005. "A 'Research' Database on Infrastructure Economic Performance." Policy Research Paper No. 3643, World Bank, Washington, DC.

Noël, P. 2009. "A Market Between US: Reducing the Political Cost of Europe's Dependence on Russian Gas." EPRG Working Paper, No. 0916. http://www.eprg. group.cam.ac.uk/wp-content/uploads/2009/06/binder13.pdf.

Pollitt, M. G. 2009. "Electricity Liberalisation in the European Union: A Progress Report." EPRG Working Paper No. 0929. http://www.eprg.group.cam.ac.uk/wp-content/uploads/2009/12/Binder1.pdf.

Price Waterhouse Coopers. 2009. *Crisis or Not, Renewable Energy Is Hot, Price Waterhouse Coopers Renewable Energy Report.* http://www.pwc.com/en_GX/gx/psrc/pdf/crisis_or_not_renewable_energy_is_hot.pdf.

Vagliasindi, M., and J. Besant-Jones. 2012. *Revisiting Policy Options on the Market Structure in the Power Sector.* Direction in Development. Washington, DC: World Bank.

CHAPTER 1

Investment Needs and Financing Challenges

The global financial crisis began with a liquidity shortfall in the U.S. banking system after the real estate bubble collapsed in 2007. By 2008, a global credit crunch had set in. Some financial institutions were bailed out by governments, investor confidence plummeted, and stock markets turned down. Both the financial crisis and the resulting economic recession hurt power sector growth and investment, which is not surprising given how vulnerable these investments are because of the large amounts of capital and long maturities that are required.

How are public-private partnerships (PPP) faring? This matters greatly because the need to expand generation capacity is expected to continue in the coming years as developing countries return to growth rates of 5 percent by 2010 and higher rates in subsequent years. It also matters because PPPs—in which the private sector can provide significant amounts of project financing—may provide budget relief to governments, as well as significant transfers of skills and know-how. With these savings, governments could invest in projects that are less amenable to PPPs. The push for privatization and PPPs from 1990 to the present has led to a large proportion of electricity services being delivered by PPPs in developing countries. In fact, since 2004, PPPs have represented the lion's share in electricity generation and distribution, particularly in middle-income countries. However, many countries have reported problems in recent years about delayed or cancelled projects, raising worries about whether PPPs are up to the job and whether the financing gaps are manageable.

To better understand what is at stake, we undertook a study to see how the impact of this recent crisis on PPP investment and financing compares with what happened in earlier crises. This chapter reviews our findings and then examines the latest projections for additional power sector investment needed in response to climate change policies and agreements—and where the money might come from. The good news is that most developing countries weathered the storm better than might have been expected, despite some setbacks. The key messages are:

- While many private electricity projects have been delayed and financing costs have increased, the impact of the global financial crisis—with 15 large projects implemented in 2009—was less severe than that of previous crises that originated in developing countries
- This resilience stems from developing countries' need to expand generation capacity, electricity sector reforms and better regulatory frameworks, packages to attract independent power producers, and short-term solutions (such as rental power plants)
- The crisis brought both short-term relief—lower electricity demand to take the pressure off supply shortages—and longer-term problems—higher financing costs for infrastructure
- The sharply reduced appetite of commercial banks for long-term financing in many countries makes international financing institutions especially valuable for private projects
- The impact of climate change on the power sector's investment needs is daunting, necessitating both public and private financing.

How the Recent Financial Crisis Compares to Past Ones

After the Asian financial crisis in 1997 and the economic recession in the early 2000s, private investment in the power sector remained reduced for several years with electricity supply exceeding demand in many countries (figure 1.1).

Figure 1.1 New Projects Have Rebounded Much More Quickly Than in the Past
electricity PPPs projects in developing countries

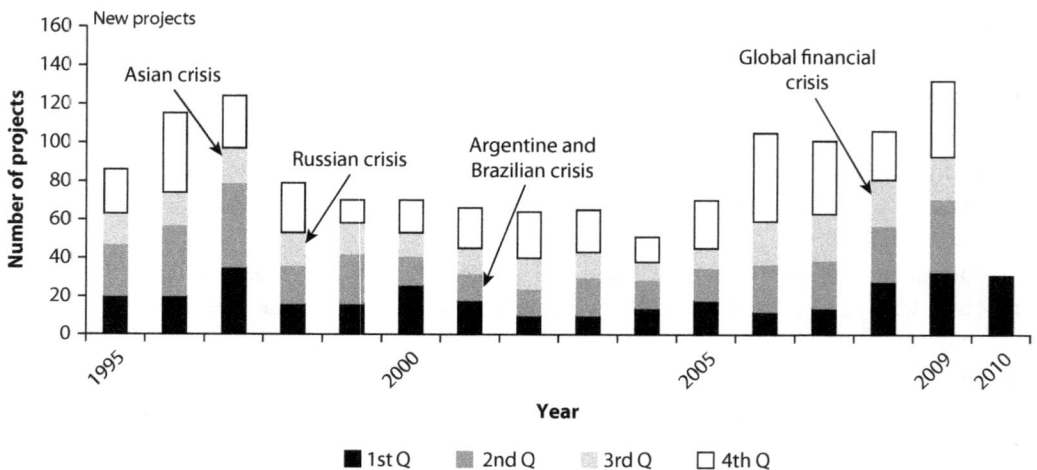

Sources: World Bank and PPIAF, PPI Project Database.

As the economies recovered, electricity demand growth rates rebounded, justifying renewed investment in generation, transmission, and distribution capacity in 2006. At the onset of the 2008 global financial crisis, investment was still lagging and many developing countries were facing the prospect of electricity supply shortfalls. Thus, the period of underinvestment resulting from the previous financial and economic crises served to attenuate the impact of the global financial crisis.

In the last quarter of 2008, during the most severe phase of the crisis, investment in electricity projects fell sharply, but it recovered strongly in 2009. After almost a decade of reduced activity, private participation in electricity has shown a strong revival in developing countries in 2007–09. Investment commitments (hereafter, *investments*) to PPP electricity projects in developing countries reached US$45.4 billion in 2007, about double that of the previous year (figure 1.2). Such a level represents an increase of over 150 percent from the level in 2004, and brings investment just 17 percent below the peak level

Figure 1.2 The Recovery Has Mainly Benefited Three Countries
investment commitments to electricity PPP projects in developing countries

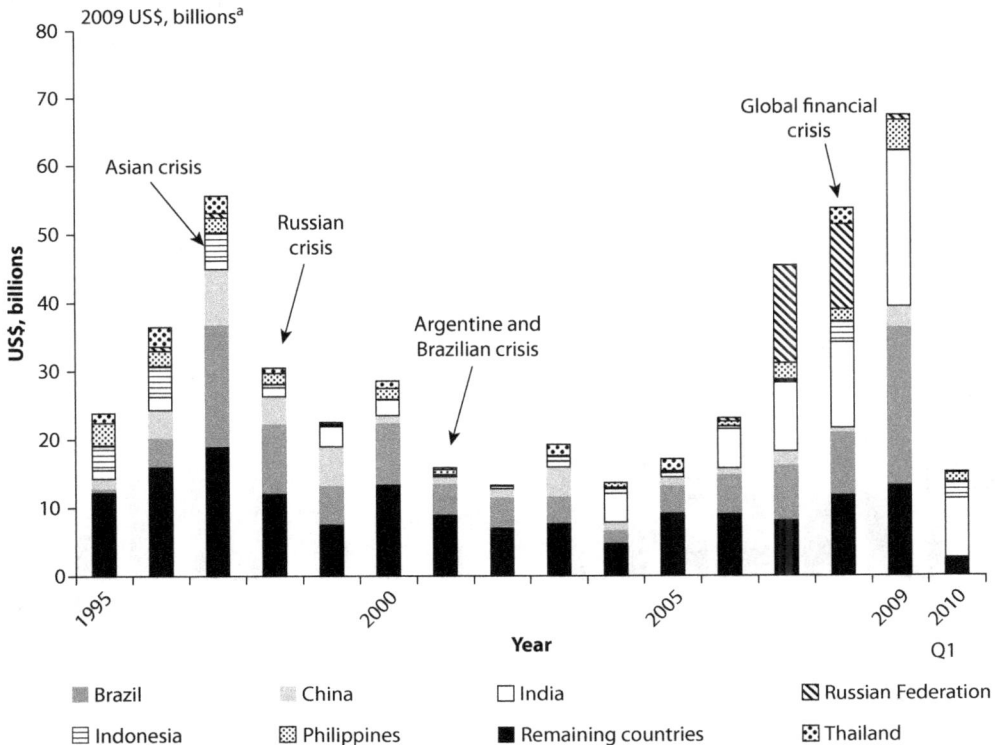

Sources: World Bank and PPIAF, PPI Project Database.
Notes: Includes additional investments in projects that reached financial or contractual closure in 1990–2009.
a. Adjusted by US CPI.

reached in 1997. Investment reached a level of US$53.5 in 2008 to a new peak of US$67.2 in 2009 after the recovery from the crisis. However, this recovery was highly selective. Three countries—Brazil, India, and the Russia—accounted for most of the growth in 2007–09. If these three are excluded, investment would have recovered at much lower pace in 2007/08 and have been less than half of the peak level reported in 1997.

The quick recovery experienced in 2009 differs from those of previous financial and economic crises. The Asian financial crisis in 1997 came after an investment boom in independent power producers (IPPs) from 1992 to 1996, when the volume of private power projects financed was three times that in all previous years. Private activity, measured by investment and number of projects, declined after the 1997 financial crisis in Asia and the 2001/02 economic crises in Argentina and Brazil, and remained reduced for many years in East Asia and Latin America (figure 1.3). Activity in the most active countries in the region such as Brazil, Indonesia, Philippines, and Thailand declined after the economic crisis experienced in their respective regions.

Most of the recent PPP investment growth has been driven by large projects—those involving investment of US$1 billion or more—a major turnaround from earlier years (figure 1.4). After the boom of private activity in the mid–1990s, no large project was implemented in 2001/02, and two to four were implemented a year in 2003–06. This trend, however, started to be

Figure 1.3 Past Crises Have Hit Originating Regions Hard

investment commitments to electricity projects in developing countries by region

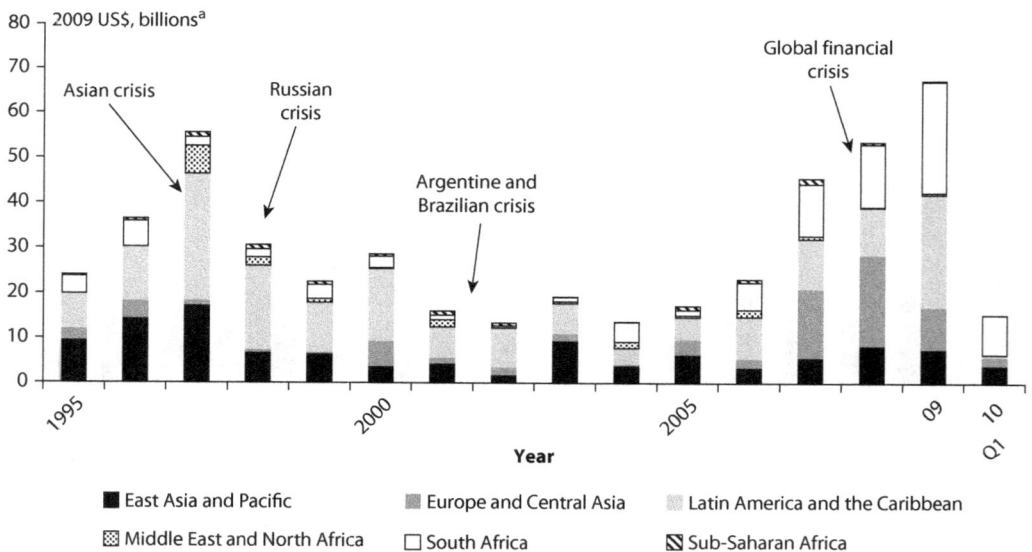

Sources: World Bank and PPIAF, PPI Project Database.
Notes: Includes additional investments in projects that reached financial or contractual closure in 1990–2009.
a. Adjusted by US CPI.

Figure 1.4 Large Projects Are Driving the Recovery

investment commitments to electricity PPP projects in developing countries by project size, 1995–2010 Q1

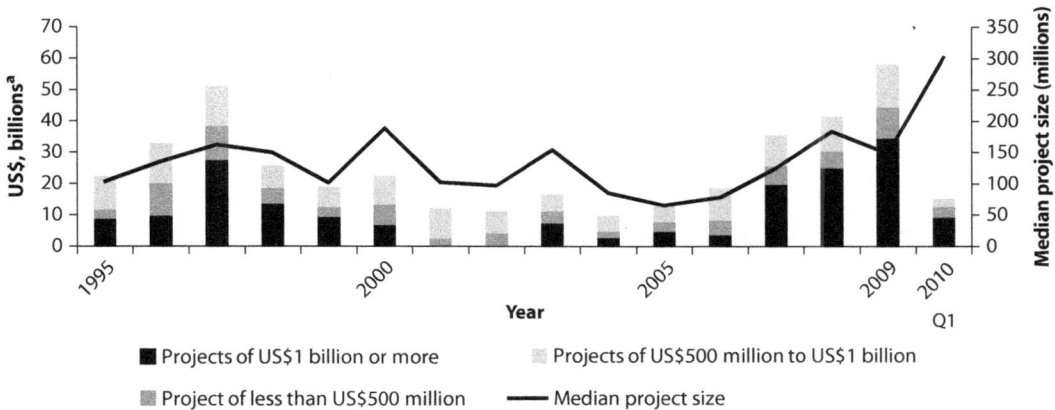

Legend:
- ■ Projects of US$1 billion or more
- ▨ Projects of US$500 million to US$1 billion
- ▨ Project of less than US$500 million
- ▬ Median project size

Sources: World Bank and PPIAF, PPI Project Database

Notes: Includes only investment commitments at financial or contractual closure. It does not include additional investment in subsequent quarters.

a. Adjusted by US CPI.

reversed in 2007 when 10 large projects were implemented. The appetite for large projects continued in 2008 when 15 projects of US$1 billion or more reached financial closure.

Despite the reduced liquidity in credit markets and more stringent lending conditions in the aftermath of the global financial crisis, 15 large projects were also implemented in 2009. Investment in projects of US$1 billion or more increased from a range of US$3 billion to US$5 billion in 2004–06 to a range of US$21 billion to US$24 billion in 2007/08 and to a peak of US$29.3 billion in the first three quarters of 2009. Investment in projects of US$500 million to US$1 billion fluctuated between US$4.6 billion and US$6.8 billion in 2006–09. Investment in projects of less than US$500 million grew from around US$5 billion in 2004/05 to a range of US$8.6 billion to US$9.6 billion in 2006–09.

Most of the projects have been new power plants in Brazil and India, and divested RAO UES power plants in Russia. Other countries that have implemented large projects include China (the partial divestiture of IPP), Indonesia (a new power plant), Philippines (the concession of the national transmission company), Romania (the divestiture of electricity distribution company), Thailand (a new power plant), and Turkey (a new power plant and divestiture of the electricity distribution company). Among the large projects, few were remarkably large—such as 3.3 gigawatts, US$5.7 billion Santo Antonio Hydro power plant and 3.3 gigawatts, US$4.17 billion Jirau Hydro power plant in Brazil, and 4.2 gigawatts, US$4.2 billion Mundra ultra mega power plant and 4 gigawatts, US$4.1 billion Sasan ultra mega power project in India. Of the remaining large projects, the biggest one was a 25-year US$2.9 billion concession of National Transmission Corporation in Philippines.

New private participation in electricity, however, has been affected by the financial crisis. A recent survey of electricity projects looking for finance or being awarded from January 2008 to September 2009 revealed that 42 of the 382 surveyed projects involving investments of US$16.9 billion have been delayed or are at risk of being delayed owing to the financial crisis, especially in South Asia (table 1.1). However, investment costs increased, and many projects were canceled, delayed, or forced to switch funding from private sources to international financial institutions.

Table 1.1 The Financial Crisis Has Hampered New PPP Investments

investment commitments to electricity projects, January 2008 to September 2009

Impact	EAP	ECA	LAC	MENA	SA	SSA	Total
			US$ millions (Number of projects)				
No severe impact							
No major impact reported	17,791 (61)	32,607 (89)	36,193 (55)	2,060 (5)	36,392 (65)	2,702 (16)	127,745 (291)
Raised financing but at a higher cost	0	0	0	0	1,375 (1)	385 (2)	1,760 (3)
Project restructuring							
Because of the crisis	0	6,338 (2)	0	0	0	0	6,338 (2)
Because of more than the crisis	0	0	100 (1)	0	0	0	100 (1)
Delayed							
Because of the crisis	0	1,153 (4)	230 (1)	0	6,038 (7)	0	7,420 (12)
Because of more than the crisis	7,842 (10)	3,910 (2)	0	0	7,167 (15)	0	18,919 (27)
For reasons other than the crisis	0	8,413 (3)	0	– (1)	1,694 (5)	300 (1)	10,407 (10)
Delayed potentially							
Because of the crisis	2,722 (3)	1,079 (2)	1,301 (5)	60 (1)	4,371 (4)	0	9,533 (15)
Because of more than the crisis	0	148 (1)	0	0	3,464 (6)	0	3,612 (7)
For reasons other than the crisis	1,150 (1)	0	0	0	1,224 (2)	0	2,374 (3)
Canceled potentially							
Because of more than the crisis	800 (1)	0	0	0	470 (1)	0	1,270 (2)
For reasons other than the crisis	0	1,100 (1)	0	0	– (2)	0	1,100 (3)
Canceled							
Because of the crisis	0	0	0	0	10 (1)	0	10
Because of more than the crisis	0	5,300 (2)	– (1)	0	305 (1)	450 (1)	6,055 (5)
Total	30,305 (76)	60,048 (106)	37,824 (63)	2,120 (7)	62,510 (110)	3,837 (20)	196,644 (382)

Source: The World Bank and PPIAF, Impact of the crisis on PPI database with private participation awarded, raising financing, or at advanced stage of tender in developing countries.

How Does the Financial Crisis Affect the Financing Gaps?

Before the global financial crisis, the power sectors of most developing countries experienced continued high growth in demand for electricity. Many countries were experiencing or nearing a supply shortage, as demand outstripped the pace at which countries were building new electricity generators or replacing ageing infrastructure in generation, transmission, and distribution.

The financial crisis brought both relief and new problems to the power sectors in developing countries facing energy crises. On the plus side, the temporary drop in demand for electricity caused by the decline in energy-intensive industries delayed or relieved some of the supply shortages. For those countries that were still able to attract and maintain investment in power infrastructure, this easing of pressure on the demand side in effect prevented an impending energy crisis and created a window of opportunity for meeting sector investment needs (World Bank 2010a). In Peru, the international financial crisis halted the rapid growth of electricity demand, which actually helped avert an energy supply crisis in 2009 and reduced pressure on generation expansion. However, the crisis also had a negative, but not critical, impact on the financing of new investments in the power sector.

For some countries, however, the financial crisis contributed to an energy crisis, because although they experienced only a short-term reduction in electricity demand, they also experienced a long-term reduction in investment in power sector infrastructure. Some electricity generation projects struggled to reach financial closure, while others were scrapped altogether. For example, Jamaica may experience a shortage in generation capacity by 2014, given that more than 150 megawatts of capacity was delayed compared to the precrisis investment plan, while the slow-down in demand was moderate.

What happened to investment needs and financial gaps in developing countries following the crisis? There is no overall estimate—and certainly it is too soon to know—but we did look at what had happened in 18 developing countries, representing all regions except Sub-Saharan Africa. We tailored the "top-down" macroeconomic approach (which estimates annual investment needs for a given growth target) and the "bottom-up" engineering approach (which estimates the one-time cost of reaching specific infrastructure goals) by incorporating revised projections for global and country specific growth. Our framework relied on two key transmission channels:

- *Macroeconomic transmission channels.* The economic slowdown affected the demand for energy services, reducing investment needs in the short run. The reduction in energy demand made it easier for countries to keep up with investment in energy supply. Investment costs decreased initially owing to the drop in fuel prices, and the pace of additional investments slowed. However, the political crisis in the Middle East that began in early 2011, as well as the March 2011 earthquake in Japan, has contributed to a rise in the price of oil—from around US$38 per barrel in 2008 to a high of US$120 in 2011, before dropping slightly. Commodity prices have also increased since early 2010. The increase in commodity and fuel prices has pushed up investment and operating costs, essentially eliminating the initial reduction in investment costs brought about by the decrease in demand for energy services.

- *Financing transmission channels*. Deterioration in revenue collection and reduced access to finance reduced profitability and availability of funds for the energy sector. The revenue collection performance of utilities deteriorated as consumers came under increasing financial pressure. As a consequence, electricity utilities in the private and the public sector were in a weaker position to implement projects. Financing became more expensive and less available in the short-term.

Overall, we found that countries have been weathering shocks of the global financial crisis significantly better than in the past through real and financial transmission channels, but there are still signs of vulnerabilities (appendix A).

Government Response to the Financial Crisis

Many countries received emergency financial assistance in the form of multilateral and bilateral loans. The World Bank provided the Kyrgyz Republic with US$11 million in emergency assistance in 2008 and US$4 million in 2009 (50 percent grant/50 percent loan) to help pay operating costs at the Bishkek combined heat and power plant (World Bank 2010a), and the country is increasingly turning to bilateral donors, such as Russia and China, to finance large power projects (World Bank 2010a). Other countries tried to counter the effects of the financial crisis through government intervention—with mixed results (box 1.1).

But in many countries, the government's ability to respond to the financial crisis has been hampered by pre-existing financing gaps in the power sector. These countries already have a backlog of financing needs for necessary repairs to transmission and generation facilities and required capacity additions to address supply shortages. The pre-existing financing gap means that the current investment gap is quite large as compared with the size of the economy (table 1.2). For example, in Armenia, the transmission infrastructure is 45-years old. A total of 520 kilometers of transmission lines are in need of urgent rehabilitation at a cost of US$80–100 million. In addition, a 600 megawatts supply gap will emerge when a nuclear plant retires in 2017 (World Bank 2010a). In total, Armenia has an investment gap for 2010–15 of almost US$6 billion, which is about half the size of the country's gross domestic product (GDP). In Indonesia, tariff reforms were curtailed in late 2003, which hurt the bankability of electricity projects (ESMAP 2010a). As a result, a financing gap had emerged even before the financial crisis occurred. On the other hand, Romania's almost US$15 billion investment gap is not out of line with the country's overall GDP.

In Sub-Saharan Africa, as elsewhere, the financial crisis exacerbated pre-existing financing challenges. A joint report by the New Partnership for

Box 1.1

Government Response to the Financial Crisis

Ukraine—Government Response to the Financial Crisis Hurts Power Sector

The financial crisis affected Ukraine's economy through a large drop in GDP, currency depreciation, fall in exports, and tighter credit. In 2009, an 8.7 percent drop in demand delayed the onset of a power supply gap from 2015 to 2017. But government intervention focused on helping other economic sectors. To support state-owned coal mines, the government required power plants to purchase coal from state mines, which hurt the financial performance of the power plants. And distribution companies were hurt by the government-imposed moratorium of tariff increases.

Most commercial lenders and private investors lacked interest in the power sector before the crisis because of the poor regulatory environment. Future involvement now seems less likely because of how the financial crisis and government intervention have affected the financial performance of utilities. As a result, IFIs and bilateral donors remain the primary source of long-term lending to the sector.

India—Fiscal Stimulus Package Helps Power Sector

The global financial crisis did not have a substantial impact on India's electric power infrastructure investments. India's power sector resilience is attributed to its strong domestic demand fundamentals, broadening of the domestic private power developer base, greater dependence on domestic sources of debt funding, existence of strong sector-focused financing entities, and appropriate monetary policy measures by the central bank to address liquidity problems. The fiscal stimulus packages in December 2008 and January 2009 played an important role as well in helping the power sector weather the financial crisis. The packages included government guaranteed funds for infrastructure spending and additional public spending on capital projects.

Source: World Bank 2010; ESMAP 2010.

Table 1.2 Some Investment Gaps Are Large because of Pre-Existing Problems

comparison of investment gap to GDP, state budget, sector revenues, and capital expenditures

(million US$)	Investment gap 2010–15	GDP 2008	State budget 2008	Gross sector revenues 2008	Total CAPEX 2006–08
Armenia	5,855	11,917	2,383	434	593
Kyrgyz Republic	3,062.2–4,062.2[a]	5,050	1,530	238	97
Romania	14,665.2[b]	200,087	64,428	No data available	
Serbia With strategic investors	3,341	24,270	12,017	2,898	263.3
Without strategic investors	6,750				
Ukraine	30,830.4	172,830	39,887	No data available	1,265

Source: World Bank 2010.
Notes: a. Options for future thermal generation include rehab of Bishkek combined heat power (CHP) (US$350 million) or construction of Kara-Keche thermal power plant (TPP) (US$1.2–1.5 billion).
b. Calculated based on total investment needs.

Africa's Development (NEPAD) and the Organization for Economic Co-operation and Development (OECD) highlights the challenges African countries face in securing financing for the power sector (NEPAD-OECD 2009). The report finds a variety of impediments. On the financial side, there are high costs inherent to the energy sector, limited access to funding, poor or non-existent sovereign credit ratings, narrow domestic capital markets, and a lack of financial instruments like project bonds. On the regulatory side, there is a lack of independent or impartial regulators, lack of competition or open access to transmission and distribution networks, weak procurement laws, one-off rather than standard power purchase agreements, inefficient or non-transparent tendering, poor contract laws, and tariffs that do not provide for inflation or cost changes. On the capacity side, there is a lack of skills to manage PPPs, inadequate local judicial systems, and regional and sub-national regulatory frameworks that are not harmonized.

Power Sector Operating Expenditures

How about the power sector's operating expenses? Evidence from past crises suggests that maintenance and operating expenditures are hit particularly hard, and this crisis is no different. Rising fuel costs and declining revenue are the main culprits. In countries that purchase fuel in foreign currency, such as Armenia and Kyrgyz Republic, fuel costs rose even higher than elsewhere as a result of a currency depreciation. In Romania, generation companies decreased their operating expenditures and employment to cope with declining revenue from electricity sales resulting from a drop in demand (World Bank 2010a).

However, in spite of the expected decline in the demand for infrastructure services, preliminary results from a simulation exercise show that maintenance needs will continue to increase. In fact, estimates to 2015 suggest that, assuming that new investment will occur though at a reduced pace, maintenance needs (in terms of GDP) in developing countries will be on average 2 percent higher than they would have been in the absence of the crisis, despite the fact that new investments needs will drop by about 12 percent because of the financial crisis and lower demand for power stemming from reduced GDP growth. This result underscores the need to safeguard maintenance resources to preserve the existing infrastructure stock as well as new investments (see SDN 2009).

Many factors explain the resilience of investment in private electricity projects:

- The demand (consumption) for electricity has grown faster than installed capacity in many developing countries in the past 15 years, creating a pressing need to expand generation capacity. In Vietnam, 3.75 gigawatts of capacity additions are required to restore reserve margins. In Indonesia, electricity demand is expected to triple by 2020.

- Many developing countries that have reformed their electricity sectors and created regulatory frameworks to put the sector on sound commercial footing have been able to attract private investment. For example, the Philippine power sector underwent major reforms in 2004 when the state-owned major power generator separated its generation and transmission assets. By the end of 2008, most large plants accounting for 48 percent of generation capacity had been successfully privatized (ESMAP 2010a).
- Some countries have focused on creating packages to attract independent power producers. Prior to the early 2000 economic crisis, Egypt successfully introduced an IPP scheme, whereby privately owned power stations entered into long-term power purchase agreements with the country's single buyer of electricity and also benefited from state guarantees (ESMAP 2010b). But the financial crisis stifled the momentum for this to occur. In Tunisia, the public utility generates 70–75 percent of the country's power and monopolizes transmission and distribution. Despite a 1996 law allowing private operators to produce electricity under public concessions, only two IPPs operate to date. However, Tunisia has attracted major developers from Europe, Asia, and the Gulf Countries to undertake two planned IPP projects that will add 1.6 gigawatts of capacity from 2011 to 2016 (ESMAP 2010c)
- Countries with power crises have resorted to short-term private solutions, such as rental power plants, to reduce the severity of blackout and power shortages (box 1.2). However, occasionally even rental power plants remain out of reach. Pakistan planned to resort to rental power plants as a quick-fix solution to the energy crisis, but was unable to secure any of the planned 2,250 megawatts of capacity in 2009 (ESMAP 2010d). In addition, old rental power plants faced natural gas shortages, forcing them to use expensive residual fuel oil instead. This led to greater fuel imports and loss of generation capacity.

Given the financial crunch and all the incomplete energy projects, there is a risk that if economic recovery is faster than projected, there might be a mismatch between demand and supply. If that occurred, policy measures would be needed to boost, energy efficiency, phase out subsidies, and protect the most vulnerable consumers (IEA *et al.* 2010).

Under-investment in a context of rapid demand growth has been a major cause of the power crisis. In some countries, supply shocks have exacerbated the situation. Supply shocks include droughts in East Africa; oil price, inflation which made it difficult for many West African countries to afford diesel imports; gas shortages owing to growing domestic demand and declining domestic production, which led to greater dependency on imported oil in Bangladesh and Pakistan; and conflicts that destroyed the power infrastructure in some fragile African states. In some countries, subsidies to the electricity sector have become a heavy burden for public finances. Electricity and petroleum subsidies represented 3 percent of GDP in Pakistan in 2008.

Box 1.2

Emergency Solutions to Power Sector Crises

A common response to the immediate crisis is to tender short-term leases for energy power, ranging from six months to three years. Unlike conventional electricity generation projects, rental projects can be put in place in a few weeks or months. However, these plants can become a large fiscal burden. Given the preponderance of small diesel units, the cost has typically been US$0.20–0.30 per kilowatt-hour, exceeding by many times the cost of electricity from longer term sources. In 2005–09, developing countries, primarily those with power crises, implemented almost 2,000 megawatts of rental power plant capacity (see figure B1.2). Pakistan commissioned 2,250 megawatts of rental power capacity in 2009, and Bangladesh commissioned 600 megawatts of rental power capacity in 2010.

Figure B1.2 Sub-Saharan Africa Relied Heavily on Rental Power

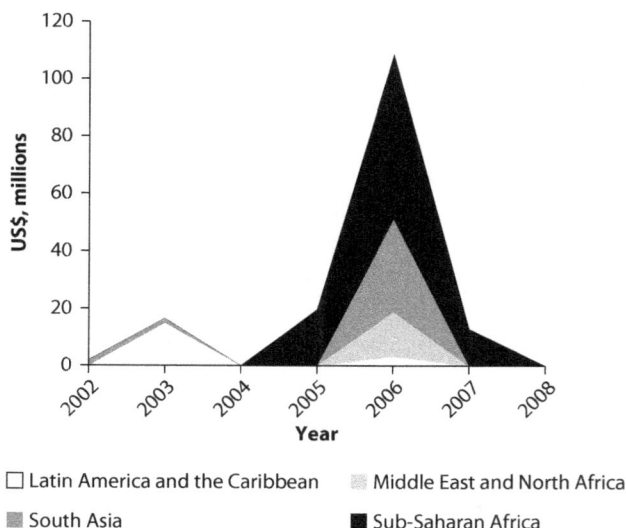

□ Latin America and the Caribbean   ▦ Middle East and North Africa
     ▨ South Asia   ■ Sub-Saharan Africa

For some countries, the price tag of emergency power generation can be high—estimated at 4.25 percent of GDP in Sierra Leone and almost 3.3 percent of GDP in Uganda (see table B1.2).

Table B1.2 Emergency Power Generation in Sub-Saharan Africa is Taking a High Financial Toll

Country	Date	Contract	Capacity	% total installed capacity	Estimated annual cost as % GDP
Kenya	2006	1 year	100	8.3	1.45
Uganda	2006	2 years	100	41.7	3.29
Sierra Leone	2007	1 year	20	133.3	4.25

Sources: AICD 2008 for data on SSA.

Sources: Vivien Foster and Cecilia Briceño-Garmendia, (2010) Africa Infrastructure: A time for transformation; Asia Pulse, December 24, 2009, 5 Rental Power Plants in Private Sector Okayed in Bangladesh; Reuters, September 17, 2009, Will Rental Power Solve Pakistan's Energy Woes?

How Do Climate Change Considerations Affect Investment Needs?

Climate Change Mitigation and Adaptation: Overall Impact

On top of conventional power needs, countries all over the world must grapple with investments to mitigate and adapt to climate change. But there is considerable uncertainty about how much this will cost in individual countries, what measures can be undertaken in both the short and longer term, and how cost-effective specific interventions are in reducing emissions.

Estimates of overall economy-wide investment needs range from US$170 to US$12,205 billion per year for mitigation and from US$75 to US$100 billion per year for adaptation over the period from 2010 to 2050 (table 1.3 and table B.1 in appendix B). The wide range reflects the uncertainty involved in making climate change projections and differing assumptions and methodologies. That said, most studies start by defining a baseline investment need for clean energy that is then supplemented with the incremental investment costs of achieving a lower carbon energy base, depending on alternative assumptions (related to the stabilization target, the pathway to stabilization, and the underlying development pathways of developing countries, including technological developments

Table 1.3 Predictions Vary Enormously on Funds Needed for Mitigating GHG Emissions

additional investment for GHG mitigation relative to business-as-usual or the reference Scenario

Date	Scenarios	Energy sector	Power sector	Regional distribution[a]
		IEA world energy outlook		
2010	**450 Policy scenario**[b] 450 Scenario (2 °C increase in global temperature)	US$11.6 trillion (2010–30) or US$580 billion/year, US$18 trillion (2010–35) or US$720 billion/year	**Power generation: (US$2,009)** US$2.4 trillion (2010–35) or US$96 billion/year	Energy 2010–35: US$7.9 trillion (OECD+) US$5.8 trillion (other major economies)
2009	**450 Policy scenario** 450 Scenario (2 °C increase in global temperature)	US$10.5 trillion (2010–30) 45% of which in transport US$525 billion/year	**Power generation: (US$2,008)** US$1.75 trillion (2010–30) US$87.5 billion/year (28% higher than the Reference scenario)	Energy 2010–30: US$5 trillion (OECD) US$3.1 trillion (other major economies)
2008	**550 Policy scenario** GHG concentration is stabilized at 550 ppm of CO_2-eq	—	**Power generation: (US$2,007)** US$1.2 trillion (2010–30) US$60.0 billion/year	Power generation 2010–30: US$170 billion (other major economies) US$890 billion (OECD+)
	450 Policy scenario GHG concentration is limited to 450 ppm CO_2-eq	—	**Power generation: (US$2,007)** US$3.6 trillion (2010–30) US$180 billion/year	Power generation 2010–30: US$1.4 trillion (other major economies) US$1.6 trillion (OECD)

(table continues on next page)

Table 1.3 Predictions Vary Enormously on Funds Needed for Mitigating GHG Emissions (continued)

Date	Scenarios	Energy sector	Power sector	Regional distribution[a]
		IEA energy technology perspectives		
2010	**BLUE scenario** Reduce CO_2 emissions by 50% from 2005 by 2050	US$46 trillion (2007–50) or US$1.1 trillion/year (1.9% of world GDP/year)	Electricity sector: (US$2,008, including T&D) **US$9.3 trillion** Power generation: US$6 trillion US$150 billion/year	—
2009	**BLUE scenario** Reduce CO_2 emissions by 50% from 2005 by 2050	US$45 trillion (2005–50) 18% over baseline US$1.1 trillion/year (1.9% of world GDP/year)	Electricity sector: (US$2,005, including T&D) **US$2.9 trillion** Power generation: US$3.6 trillion (28%↑) US$80 billion/year	—
2008	**ACT scenario** Bring global CO_2 emissions back to current levels by 2050	US$17 trillion (2005–50) 7% over baseline (254t) US$400 billion/year (0.7% of world GDP/year)	Electricity sector: (US$2,005, including T&D) US$-1.1 trillion Power generation: US$0.7 trillion (6%↑) US$15.6 billion/year	—

Source: World Bank data.

Notes: — = not available.

a. All the countries are categorized into 3 groups: OECD+ countries (OECD countries and non-OECD countries that are members of the EU), Other Major Economies (Brazil, China, the Middle East, Russia, and South Africa which are large emitters and whose GDP/cap is expected to exceed US$13,000 in 2020), and Other Countries.

b. 450 Parts per Million (ppm) CO_2-equivalent is the long-term GHG concentration limit. The trajectory is an overshoot one where GHG concentrations peak at 510 in 2035 and stay steady for about 10 years and then decline to 450 ppm.

and adoption of different policies). They also target holding global warming below the 2 degree threshold identified by the UN Intergovernmental Panel on Climate Change (IPCC) as financially and environmentally manageable.

Impact of the Financial Crisis

Most studies draw on a global GHG abatement cost curve first produced by McKinsey in January 2007 and revised in January 2009 (McKinsey 2007, 2009). It has formed the basis for discussing the cost of existing mitigation levers, such as greater energy efficiency and various types of renewable energy. In the case of Mexico, Latin America's largest fossil-fuel consuming country, a World Bank low-carbon country study shows that a variety of levels could be used to sharply cut GHG emissions, especially in agriculture and forestry, transport, and electric power sectors (box 1.3).

In August 2010, McKinsey updated the abatement cost curve to reflect the impact of the global financial crisis (McKinsey 2010). The new curve shows that business-as-usual (BAU) emissions projections for 2030 have decreased by 6 percent, owing to the 2008 global financial crisis and slowdown in economic growth. The biggest drop, 6–11 percent, is in emissions projections for developed countries, while projections for China and the rest of developing Asia

Box 1.3

A Low Carbon Growth Path for Mexico

Over the past two years, Brazil, China, India, Indonesia, Mexico, and South Africa have initiated studies—with the World Bank's Energy Sector Management Assistance Program (ESMAP)—to assess development priorities in conjunction with GHG mitigation opportunities, and to estimate additional costs and benefits of lower carbon growth. Besides strengthening country ownership of mitigation strategies, the studies have already provided two valuable outputs, in terms of a framework for establishing low carbon pathways and in terms of a knowledge and data set, which can be used as a toolkit for other countries to reduce GHG emissions and lower mitigation costs.

In the case of Mexico, Latin America's largest fossil fuel-consuming country, its study sheds insights on prospective low carbon "wedges"—which are composed of specific interventions across the key emission sectors (electric power, oil and gas, stationary energy end-use, transport, and agriculture and forestry). Three criteria were used to select interventions

Figure B1.3 Targeted Interventions Would Sharply Lower Emissions

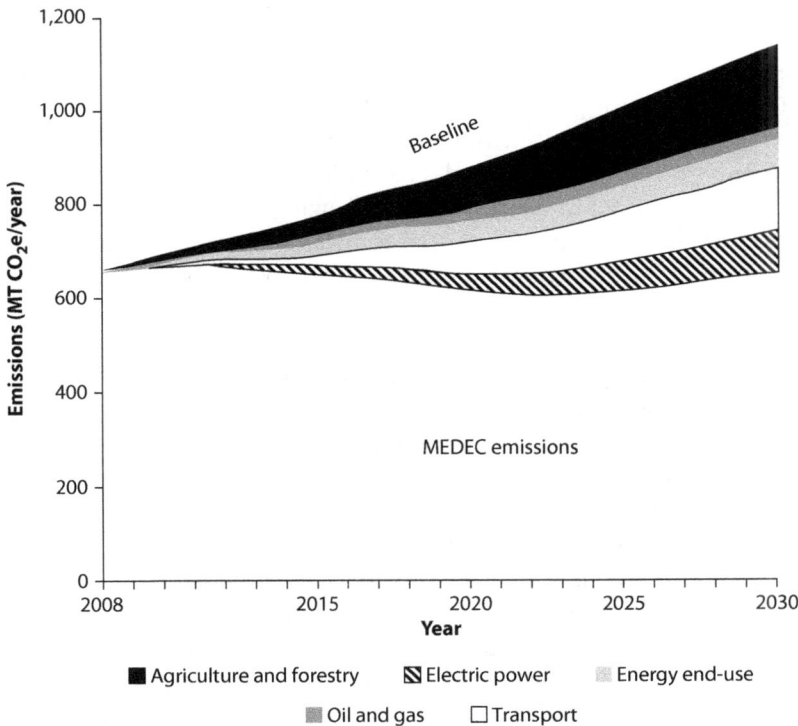

Source: World Bank data.

Note: MEDEC stands for the 2009 study, México: Estudio sobre la Disminución de Emisiones de Carbono.

(box continues on next page)

Box 1.3 A Low Carbon Growth Path for Mexico *(continued)*

(1) substantial potential for reducing emissions (the threshold was 5 Metric ton (Mt) CO_2e over the 2009–30 implementation period); (2) low economic and financial costs (either with positive economic rates of return or with carbon costs of US$25 per tCO_2e or less); and (3) feasible in the short or medium term. The study did not assume a value for carbon mitigation but rather produced a "cost of carbon" as an output, calculating the net present value as of 2008 of the direct economic costs and benefits of each intervention between 2009 and 2030 to reach the "net costs" of reducing emissions.

Under the baseline scenario, total CO_2e emissions would grow from 659 Mt in 2008 to 1,137 Mt in 2030. But under a low carbon growth path (which includes 40 interventions), total CO_2e emissions would drop by about 477 Mt in 2030 relative to the baseline—which would be virtually the same as in 2008, despite significantly higher GDP and per capita income. This estimate is still conservative, in that other interventions and technological change are not considered. The key sector is agriculture and forestry, where interventions would include reforestation, commercial plantations, and measures to reduce emissions from deforestation and forest degradation. The next most important is transport, followed by electric power, energy end-use, and oil and gas.

---

were revised upward by 1–2 percent (figure 1.5). BAU emissions projections from the power sector globally decreased by 5 percent.

Of course, reduced BAU emissions will help countries achieve their reduction targets, but the credit-constrained economic environment will likely make financing of abatement measures more challenging (McKinsey 2010). The revision suggests that abatement potential remains stable at 38 gigatons of CO_2 equivalent in 2030 through technical measures costing below €80 (US$114) per ton of CO_2 equivalent (McKinsey 2010).

Climate Change Mitigation and Adaptation: Power Sector Impact

How about the additional cost of climate change for the power sector? The International Energy Agency (IEA) provides estimates of the impact of carbon mitigation activities on power sector investment in two annual reports, the World Energy Outlook (WEO) and Energy Technology Perspectives (ETP). The key difference between them is that the WEO makes projections only for the 2010–30 period, while ETP expands the period to 2050 (table 1.3).

The estimates show that reducing CO_2 emissions by 50 percent from 2005 levels by 2050 will require investments in the electricity sector (from 2010 to 2050) of US$9.3 trillion—40 percent higher than in the baseline scenario (BLUE Scenario of ETP 2010). Of this amount, investment in power generation accounts for US$6 trillion, transmission for US$1.7 trillion, and distribution for US$1.6 trillion. Interestingly, the *additional* investment in the whole power sector is expected to be smaller than what would be expected from the increased investment in power generation alone. This is mainly because impacts from

Figure 1.5 The Financial Crisis Resulted in Lower GHG Emissions

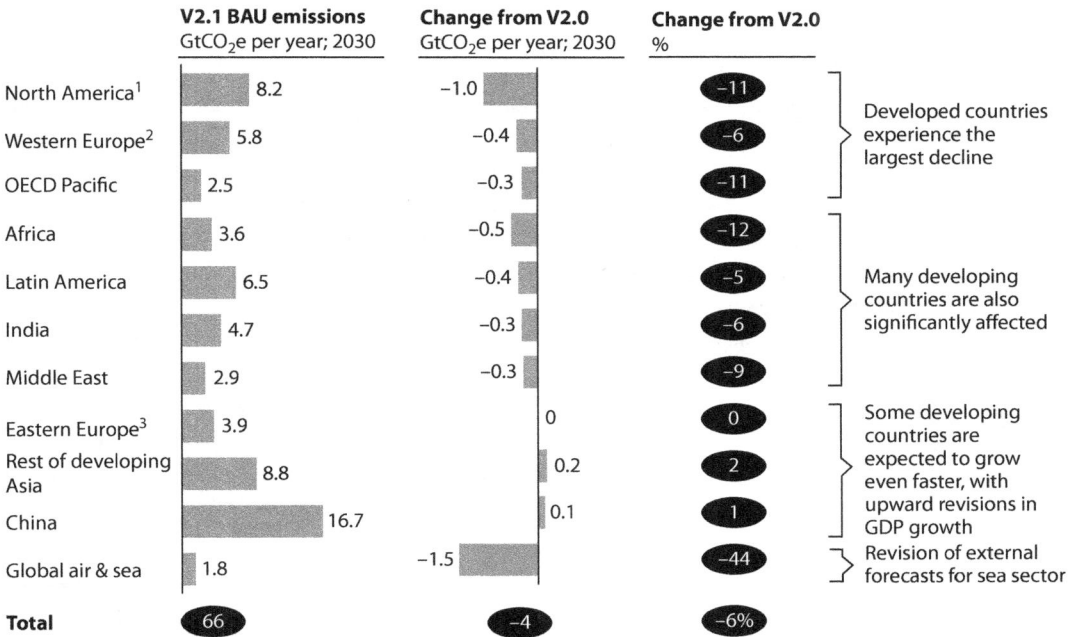

	V2.1 BAU emissions GtCO₂e per year; 2030	Change from V2.0 GtCO₂e per year; 2030	Change from V2.0 %	
North America[1]	8.2	−1.0	−11	Developed countries experience the largest decline
Western Europe[2]	5.8	−0.4	−6	
OECD Pacific	2.5	−0.3	−11	
Africa	3.6	−0.5	−12	Many developing countries are also significantly affected
Latin America	6.5	−0.4	−5	
India	4.7	−0.3	−6	
Middle East	2.9	−0.3	−9	
Eastern Europe[3]	3.9	0	0	Some developing countries are expected to grow even faster, with upward revisions in GDP growth
Rest of developing Asia	8.8	0.2	2	
China	16.7	0.1	1	
Global air & sea	1.8	−1.5	−44	Revision of external forecasts for sea sector
Total	66	−4	−6%	

1. United States and Canada.
2. Includes EU27, Andorra, Iceland, Lichtenstein, Monaco, Norway, San marino, and Switzerland.
3. Russia and non-OECD Eastern Europe.

Source: McKinsey 2010.

reducing CO_2 emissions will partly come from energy saving. By reducing demands for electricity, less investment will be required for networks, mainly distribution, compared with the reference scenarios.

As for the energy sector—which includes industry, transport, and buildings next to the power sector—the IEA estimates that there will need to be an additional investment of US$1.1 trillion per year, which is 1.9 percent of the 2009 world total GDP (IEA 2010). On a regional basis, OECD countries are expected to bear the largest share, especially before 2020. Quantitatively, the estimated size of the impact depends largely on the design of scenarios and associated assumptions on baseline emissions, projected future international climate agreements and national policies, and mitigation trajectories.

Adaptation

The power sector will play a key role in a country's ability to adapt, because without a well-functioning power sector that gives the entire population reliable access to electricity, many of the technologies that facilitate adaptation in the agriculture, infrastructure, and health sectors cannot be implemented.

Estimates of adaptation investment needs vary greatly because of differing methods, levels of inclusion (impacts and regions analyzed), and assumptions about the rate of climate change and time preferences (table B.1 in appendix B).

Box 1.4

Cost of Developing Countries Adapting to Climate Change

So how much would it cost the developing countries to adapt to climate change? A recent World Bank study puts the total at between US$75 to US$100 billion a year by 2050, assuming a temperature rise of about 2 °C. The bulk of the funds would go for infrastructure, protection of coastal zones, and water supply and flood protection. On a regional basis, the largest burden would fall on East Asia and Pacific, followed by Latin America and the Caribbean, and the lowest burden would fall on the Middle East and North Africa. But Africa would have the highest cost relative to GDP.

The study looks at two climate change scenarios to capture as large as possible a range of model predictions yielding extremes of dry and wet climate projections. It finds that in a "drier" one, costs would be significantly lower than in a "wetter" one, largely because the latter would lead to more infrastructure deterioration, which would steeply increase investment needs. But both scenarios show costs increasing over time, although falling as a percentage of GDP—suggesting that economic growth lowers vulnerability to climate change.

Source: Economics of Adaptation to Climate Change 2009.

A 2007 study by the UN Framework Convention on Climate Change (UNFCCC) estimates global investment needs at US$50–170 billion annually between 2010 and 2030 (table B.1 in appendix B). Based on the McKinsey global GHG abatement cost curve, Project Catalyst (2009) estimates that developing countries need around US$13–25 billion annually between 2010 and 2030 to adapt to climate change.

As part of the preparations for the Copenhagen conference on extending the Kyoto Protocol, the World Bank was asked to estimate the cost of adapting to climate change in developing countries from 2010 to 2050. The Economics of Adaptation to Climate Change (EACC) study makes use of panel data for more than 160 countries for 1960–2005, projecting infrastructure demand at five year intervals from 2010 to 2050. The cost of adaptation is estimated at US$75–100 billion annually between 2010 and 2050 and is divided into (1) the net increase in the cost of constructing infrastructure under some baseline scenario; (2) the net change in demand for infrastructure owing to higher temperatures or different patterns of precipitation; and (3) the net change in the costs of operating, maintaining, and replacing infrastructure (box 1.4).

Sources of Financing of Investment for Conventional Power

So who will pay for the needed investments in the power sector, beginning with investment needed for conventional power. Keep in mind that investment costs for power projects can easily run into billions of dollars, and the payback period can extend beyond 10 years. Thus, it can be difficult even for well-performing power companies to secure financing, let alone companies in poorly regulated environments. In theory, governments and power companies can finance investment in generation, transmission, and distribution through a variety of ways, from local or international banks and private equity to international financial institutions and bilateral donors. Exactly how much is available and from where typically depends on the political stability of the country, the development of the financial sector, and the regulatory and tariff regime of the power sector.

But the global financial crisis has altered the picture, with traditional funding sources to public power projects—including government budgetary transfers, internal cash generation, commercial banks, and bond markets—drying up. Government budgetary transfers have diminished owing to competing expenditure priorities. Foreign bank loans have declined and become more expensive, while local banks are liquid but constrained by single borrower limits. Most top tier foreign banks have capped funding levels, which will hurt foreign currency borrowing programs of state-owned power utilities that are seeking private finance beyond multilateral funding. And public aid flows from bilateral and multilateral donors and international financial institutions (IFIs) have decreased.

At this point, state-owned entities (SOEs) are struggling to cope with higher borrowing costs. Spreads over global benchmarks have widened for SOE borrowing, and the spreads are also higher for local loans. When combined with local currency devaluation, it has led to an erosion of SOE borrowing capacity. Most SOE borrowings are in the form of bilateral and multilateral hard currency loans. Combined with floating rate local and foreign currency loans, unhedged foreign currency and interest rate exposure could impair SOE ability to service debt. Sector lending limits are being approached. In Indonesia, state-owned banks are willing to exceed these limits but only in return for explicit government guarantees.

In some countries, commercial banks preferred to extend credit to public sector entities over private sector projects during the financial crisis. In India, power entities owned by the state governments did not face many challenges in securing debt financing, even though they are known for their relatively weaker financial profile as compared with power entities that are privately owned (ESMAP 2010d).

Sources of Financing of Investment in Period of Crisis

Recourse-Based/Own Funds. Power sector companies with strong balance sheets and robust cash flows were able to finance their investments on a recourse basis (that is, on the strength of their balance sheets). This was the case for government-owned power sector entities in India. However, the cost of borrowing went up by about 75–100 basis points in tandem with the increase in prime lending rates of banks in the immediate aftermath of the financial crisis (ESMAP 2010d).

In many developing countries, the regulatory regime of the power sector does not allow for full and predictable recovery of capital expenditure costs (including financing costs) over several years. The lack of reliable revenue means that power sector entities have a relatively weaker financial profile, ruling out financing through own funds.

Where electricity tariffs remain below cost-recovery levels, power companies are unlikely to be able to borrow at competitive rates either through the bank credit route or the bond finance route. Revenues have also been hurt by rising fuel costs, and in some cases, government intervention. In Armenia, the government waived the return on assets for state-owned utilities for 2009 and 2010, limiting revenues available for investment. In 2010, the Romanian government reduced the profit available for reinvestment from 40 percent to 10 percent for Transelectrica, the transmission and system operator (World Bank 2010a). Governments in many countries recognize the need to raise electricity tariffs to keep power companies running and make financing power sector projects more attractive. But they must gauge the level of cost pass-through consumers can bear in an economic crisis.

As external financing became unavailable, some SOEs drew upon their cash reserves to fund capital investment. For example, a large SOE in the Vietnam power sector saw its cash balance fall during the first nine months of 2008 despite liquidation of its short-term investments to offset the contracting debt market. Large SOEs have shown lower levels of tangible asset formation during the second half of 2008 and have had to slow construction on projects.

International Commercial Banks. Loan syndication remains a serious issue. Most top-tier foreign banks are focusing on lending to well-prepared projects offering significant risk cover, and many second-tier banks are unwilling to take any significant emerging country risk without an extensive security package or credit enhancement. This is the case in Bangladesh, where syndication markets dried up during the financial crisis.

Since the beginning of the crisis, interest margins have multiplied by at least two or three times because of higher liquidity costs for the banks and reassessed risk premiums (ESMAP 2010e). In China, real interest rates have increased from a negative 0.1 percent in 2007 to a positive 6 percent 2009, and in Argentina, from a negative 2.8 percent to a positive 5.2 percent—although in India, rates have gone down from 6.9 percent to 4.3 percent (table 1.4).

In addition, maturities have shortened, with project finance tenors increasing from less than 10 years, mostly through "mini perms," which allow for durations of around 12 years. In Vietnam, for example, a large independent power producer has seen maturities increase by four years for its foreign currency debt, resulting in higher debt service requirements.

In general, all deal parameters have tightened: reduced leverage (up to 25–30 percent equity instead of 20 percent for a typical power project), higher upfront fees, tighter coverage ratios, stricter covenants, and requests for reinforced support from host governments (ESMAP 2010e). For many countries—such as those in the Middle East and North Africa—risk mitigation coverage from development financial institutions, export credits, or the insurance market is a must.

Table 1.4 Real Interest Rates Have Typically Risen
pre- and postcrisis real interest rates, in percent

	2007	2008	2009
Argentina	−2.8	0.3	5.2
Armenia	12.7	8.0	17.1
Bangladesh	8.6	7.0	7.6
Bolivia	0.5	3.2	15.1
China	−0.1	−2.3	6.0
India	6.9	6.2	4.3
Kenya	7.6	1.9	7.6
Kyrgyz Republic	9.1	−1.9	20.5
Nigeria	11.6	4.1	19.1
Paraguay	13.4	11.2	28.4
Philippines	5.5	1.2	5.9
Romania	0.3	3.1	10.1
United States	4.5	2.8	2.3

Source: World Bank 2011.

In Vietnam and Indonesia, where uncovered loans are no longer a possibility, sovereigns are reviewing their ability to take on contingent liabilities on behalf of their SOEs.

Export credit agencies. Export credit agencies are critical in many deals, since they allow for loans at relatively unchanged margins with long maturities, which are difficult to find in the commercial market (ESMAP 2010e). Maturities can reach up to 12 years for fossil fuel power plants and up to 18 years for renewable energy and nuclear plants. While banks have increased their margins on these agencies' covered loans, they are still much lower than for pure commercial deals.

International financial institutions. The dramatically decreasing appetite of commercial banks for long-term financing in non-investment grade or low-investment grade countries makes international financial institutions (IFIs) especially valuable for private projects (ESMAP 2010e). They can provide additional funding and help more banks to join deals through IFI coverage schemes.

IFI funds for private projects are more expensive than before the crisis, but remain much less costly than funds from commercial banks. IFI funds now cost typically 200–250 basis points for 10–15 years, up from 100 to 125 basis points before the crisis. Currently, commercial banks provide funds for over 400 basis points, provided they accept to provide funds beyond 7–10 years (ESMAP 2010e).

The financial crisis has not limited IFI's abilities to finance investments in the power sector nor has it decreased power sector companies' appetite for concessional financing (World Bank 2010a). However, tightened fiscal space may limit governments' ability to borrow. State budget deficits in each of the countries analyzed in these studies are expected to remain above precrisis levels for the next several years.

Local Banks. In most developing countries, the local banking market is ill equipped to provide long-term finance beyond five to seven years. Larger loans require syndication among multiple local lenders, but the local market is often unable to absorb multiple large transactions concurrently (ESMAP 2010f). In Pakistan and the Philippines, the exposure of local banks to the power sector is too high to provide further credit to the sector. In Tunisia, owing to the limited size of Tunisian banks, it would be difficult for the local banking system alone to finance project amounts of several hundred million dollars (ESMAP 2010c).

Even in countries with a relatively well developed banking sector, local banks are unable to finance large power sector projects because of a shortage of foreign currency lending. In Morocco, the banking sector is well developed with structural excess liquidity, the electricity sector is seen as a good risk by the local banks, and long maturities (beyond 12 years) are still easily available on the local market. However, there is a limited availability of foreign currency on the local market. Thus, the long-term (15–18 years) foreign currency loans that will be needed to finance part of the upcoming IPPs must be made by international banks, export credit agencies, and IFIs.

Bilateral Donors. For many developing countries, donors remain the primary source of financing for the power sector, but they are capping exposure limits and lowering maturities. Russia, China, and India are active bilateral donors because of their pre-existing political and economic ties to recipient countries and their expertise in working in developing countries.

- Russia is active in neighboring East Central Asian countries, such as Armenia, the Kyrgyz Republic, and Ukraine through loans or joint ventures between Russian companies and governments
- China is funding the 360 megawatts expansion of the Kariba North Bank hydropower plant in Zambia, along with the Development Bank of Southern Africa. The China-owned Sino Hydro Corporation is the sole project contractor, taking full responsibility for construction, including the supply of materials and labor (NEPAD 2009). Here, the bilateral donor has the option of importing labor and supplies to construct the power plant, thereby reducing some of the risk if forced to hire and buy locally.
- India Eximbank is funding a US$50 million loan for Zambia to build the 150 megawatts Itezhi-Teszhi hydro power station, a joint venture between Zesco and Tata Holdings (NEPAD 2009). The project is expected to be operational by 2012.

Private Equity. Private investment is a possible source of financing for power projects, but it is harder to secure now. In Romania, many private investors were interested in renewable energy as well as thermal energy projects. Since the crisis, interest in thermal projects has waned, as the sector is restructuring, but interest in renewable energy projects continued owing to the perceived regulatory stability of EU regulations and the green certificate scheme (World Bank 2010a).

In the Philippines, privatization of the National Power Corporation (NPC), the major state-owned utility, began in 2004, but has slowed because of the financial crisis. The sale of most remaining NPC generation assets has failed, such as the privatization of Calaca worth US$748 million (ESMAP 2010a).

The risk allocation among project counterparts is important to secure funding—with developers wanting to pass more risk to governments, at the possible expense of profitability (ESMAP 2010e). Projects with more demand uncertainty, such as those with a partial off-take agreement or export uncertainty, are less competitive in accessing project finance. Willing lenders, if any, will put a risk premium on such projects, which translates into higher electricity tariffs (ESMAP 2010e).

Bond Markets. Power companies have turned to local bond markets to raise finance, but these markets are often not a viable alternative because they are largely illiquid and offer relatively short maturities. Access to global bond markets is limited to creditworthy SOEs, of which there are few, and even then, the parameters are tighter.

In Peru, Kallpa, a private generator, was able to reach financial closure in 2009 for a US$400 million thermoelectric project, using a project finance scheme (World Bank 2010b). However, Kallpa had to increase the equity contribution to 30 percent (from 25 percent precrisis) for a US$105 million, 10-year term loan. It also issued corporate bonds in the domestic market for US$172 million, 12.5 years, and a fixed rate of 8.5 percent, which was about 200 basis points above rates of similar bonds issued in mid-2007 by other large generators (World Bank 2010b).

Sources of Financing of Investment for Climate Change

When it comes to financing investment for climate change mitigation, there are additional sources on top of the traditional ones available for conventional power sector projects. Renewable energy and energy efficiency projects have access to carbon market finance and subsidies or feed-in tariffs. In addition, multilateral donors, IFIs, and private investors may prioritize investment in renewable over conventional power projects. However, renewable energy projects tend to be more expensive and more risky than conventional power projects.

Given the huge amounts needed for coping with climate change, where will this money come from? Project Catalyst (2009) estimates that of the €65–€100 billion (US$95–146 billion) annual investment needs for developing countries from 2010 to 2020, about half could be supplied by the European Union Emission Trading Scheme (ETS) markets (figure 1.6). Up to 80 percent of the funds would go toward mitigation activities with the remainder earmarked for adaptation activities.

A report by the UN Secretary General's High-Level Advisory Group on Climate Change Finance, which explores sources for raising US$100 billion per year from 2020 for climate change, suggests the financing could come from public funds, carbon market offsets, international private investment, and multilateral development banks (IEA et al. 2010). It concludes that raising this

Figure 1.6 Potential Sources of Climate Change Financing for Developing Countries

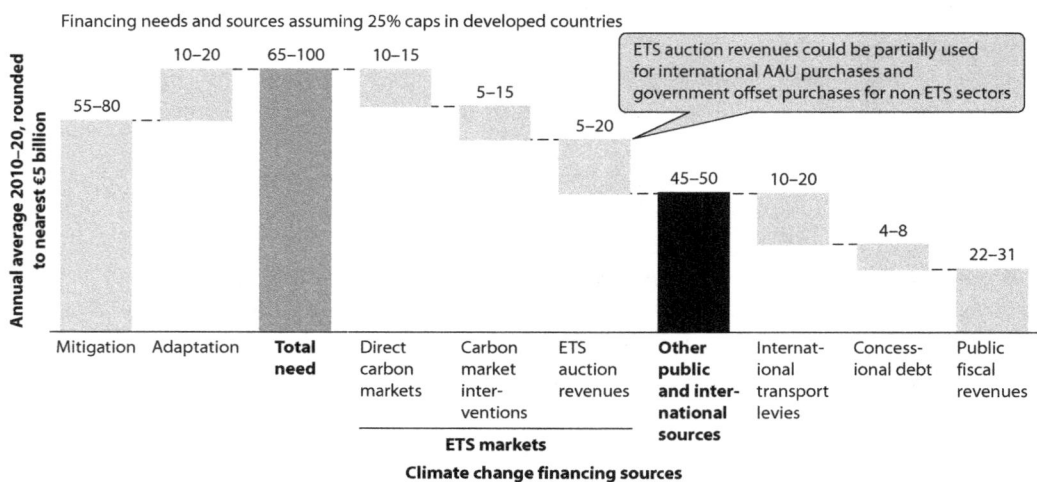

Source: Project Catalyst 2009.
Note: Estimates based on the McKinsey global greenhouse gas abatement cost curve (McKinsey 2009).

amount is feasible, but not easy, and very unlikely if it is understood to refer to public funds only. Such findings were confirmed by a new report recently submitted to the Group of 20 (World Bank 2011).

Public Funds. Public funds, mainly through public carbon market revenues, could supply about US$50 billion per year in climate change financing to developing countries. Based on a carbon price of US$25 per ton in 2020, flows to developing countries might include US$30–40 billion from auctioning all domestic rights to emit (or taxing carbon), assuming 10 percent of total revenues are allocated to developing countries. If broad carbon pricing is not feasible, an alternative may be provided by "feebates" imposing taxes (fees) on relatively emission intensive firms or on products with low energy efficiency. In addition, taxes on international aviation and shipping could supply US$10 billion, assuming 33–50 percent are earmarked for developing countries (who can also keep their own revenues from this source). Other instruments, such as redeployment of energy subsidies or a financial transaction tax, could amount to US$10 billion. Actual estimates of 2020 revenue potential for new public instruments are sensitive to many assumptions, particularly the carbon price and the share allocated to international climate finance.

Despite the recent slowdown in market activity, carbon markets showed resilience to the global financial crisis, registering US$142 million in 2010, US$2 million below the record achieved in 2009, but still more than twice the 2007 level and 6 percent higher than in 2008 (figure 1.7). The EU Emission Trading Scheme (ETS) accounts for the bulk of the activities.

Carbon Market Offsets. These offsets could provide about US$20–100 billion in flows to developing countries, according to World Bank (2011) estimates,

Figure 1.7 Carbon Markets Held up during the Financial Crisis

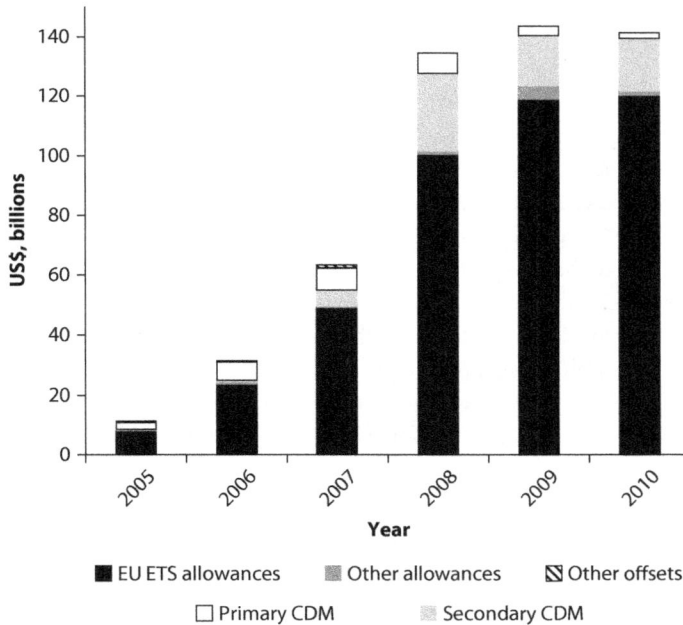

Source: World Bank 2011.
Note: EU ETS stands for European Union Eon Trading Scheme. CDM stands for Clean Development Mechanism.

although for the first time, this component of the carbon market declined slightly in 2010. Here, offsets refer to private entities or governments in developed countries purchasing project-based offsets (that is, certified emission reduction credits [CERs]) from private entities in developing countries, such as through the Clean Development Mechanism (CDM). However, the US$7 billion invested each year so far through the CDM has been concentrated mainly in emerging market economies (EC 2011). In fact, about 91 percent of CERs were earned in only four host countries: China (57 percent), India (15 percent), the Republic of Korea (11 percent), and Brazil (8 percent) (UNFCCC 2011). The European Commission is committed to achieving a better geographical balance and increasing finance for the poorest countries (EC 2011).

Private Investment. The private sector can also play a key role in financing energy efficiency investments. In fact, the AGF and World Bank (2011) identify international private investment as essential for the transition to a low-carbon and climate-resilient future. A carbon price of US$20–25 could generate around US$10–20 billion in private net capital flows. In addition, US$30–50 billion could be generated in increased carbon market flows, delivering around US$10 billion of net transfers. Assuming that energy is appropriately priced, much of this funding is expected to come from consumers and private sources. That said, public funding may be required to address market barriers like information gaps and to facilitate a buy-down in transaction costs.

As for adaptation, the expected role and sequencing of private finance is even trickier. Many of the activities will need to be embedded in development programs, ensuring that future development investments are sufficiently "climate proofed." The private sector, in some highly exposed areas, might be expected to cooperate. At this stage, however, few private investors feel they have the information to effectively factor future climate risks into decision making. The public sector would be left with a leading role, at least in the early stages of expansion: a massive public investment push, coupled in the short term with appropriate subsidy mechanisms to offset high initial prices and targeted at the most promising technology options.

A key factor inhibiting international bank participation in renewable energy in emerging countries is that the regulatory risk, which is seen as more critical in renewable than conventional energy, is often considered too high (ESMAP 2010e). A 300 megawatts wind power project in Ukraine's Crimea region was delayed because a foreign equity sponsor pulled out in 2009 (World Bank 2010a). In Armenia, small hydropower projects have become less attractive because of increased financing costs, and some commercial banks, which committed to IFI-funded small hydropower projects, are seeking co-financing sources in Armenian drams (World Bank 2010a). However, in Romania, investments in renewable energy are continuing because the market is perceived as less risky than the conventional energy one thanks to EU requirements and the green certificate trading scheme (World Bank 2010a). But investments in conventional thermal projects have been delayed or cancelled as investors wait to see how generation restructuring will affect the sector (World Bank 2010a).

Multilateral Development Banks. Finally, for every US$10 billion in paid-in capital, multilateral development banks could deliver US$30–40 billion in gross flows, resulting in US$11 billion in net flows to developing countries, according to AGF estimates. However, development banks were also hit by the global financial crisis. In Jamaica, the Inter-American Development Bank, along with PetroCaribe, scaled back its funding of non-wind renewable energy and energy efficiency programs from US$150 to US$20 million over 2010–17 (World Bank 2010b).

Investment Trends in Renewable Energy

Overall, around US$257 billion was invested globally in renewable energy in 2011. Of that, China led the way (for the third consecutive year) with new financial investments of US$52 billion (figure 1.8). Ambitious, mandatory targets for wind and solar power and the ample availability of credit in China have been the primary engines of that nation's clean energy growth. The United States came in second at about US$50 billion, and Italy managed a distant third, thanks to a newly designed solar feed-in tariff and a major Initial Public Offering (IPO) by Enel Green Power, which raised US$0.5 billion in 2010.

Figure 1.8 China Leading the Way in Investing in Renewable Energy
new financial investment in renewable energy, 2011, US$ billion

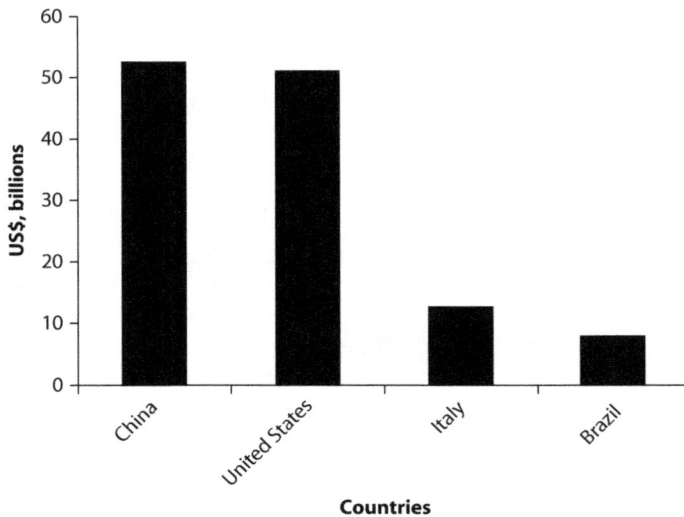

Source: Bloomberg New Energy Finance.

Among developing countries in top world positions, Brazil and India stand out. But while Brazil's renewable investment was characterized by a subdued performance, mainly owing to consolidation in the biofuel segment, India's grew strongly, supported by an accelerated depreciation tax break (expected to be reformed in 2012), new solar mission, and launch of Renewable Energy Certificates. Mexico's renewable investments increased by fourfold from 2009, reaching more then US$2.3 billion, thanks to new funding for wind projects. Egypt, the top country in the Middle East and North Africa region, achieved renewable investments of over US$1.3 billion, owing to large solar thermal and wind projects. Kenya, the top performer in Sub-Saharan Africa, invested US$1.3 billion—up from virtually zero before—on a diversified basis (wind, geothermal, small hydro, and biomass).

Stimulus packages of countries leading efforts in clean energy also included a substantial component of clean energy, both in absolute and percent of GDP terms (figure 1.9). At the height of the global financial crisis, the United States announced a US$68 billion stimulus package, and China, a generous US$46 billion.

Which types of renewable energy are drawing the most new investment? Solar power leads the way, growing at an exponential rate in 2011, mainly fueled by growth in developed countries, which recorded US$90 billion more investment than developing countries (figure 1.10). Wind power comes in second—mainly driven by developing countries—although investment is down from the peak recorded in 2010. Biomass comes in third, followed by biofuel, small hydro, geothermal, and marine.

Figure 1.9 Recent Stimulus Packages Favor Green Investments

stimulus packages, 2009

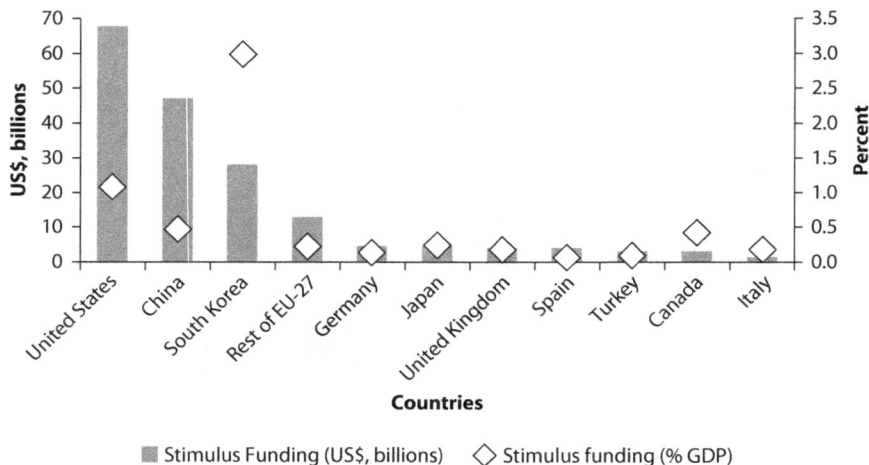

■ Stimulus Funding (US$, billions) ◇ Stimulus funding (% GDP)

Source: Bloomberg New Energy Finance.

Figure 1.10 Most New Renewable Energy Investment Going into Solar Power

(% by country)

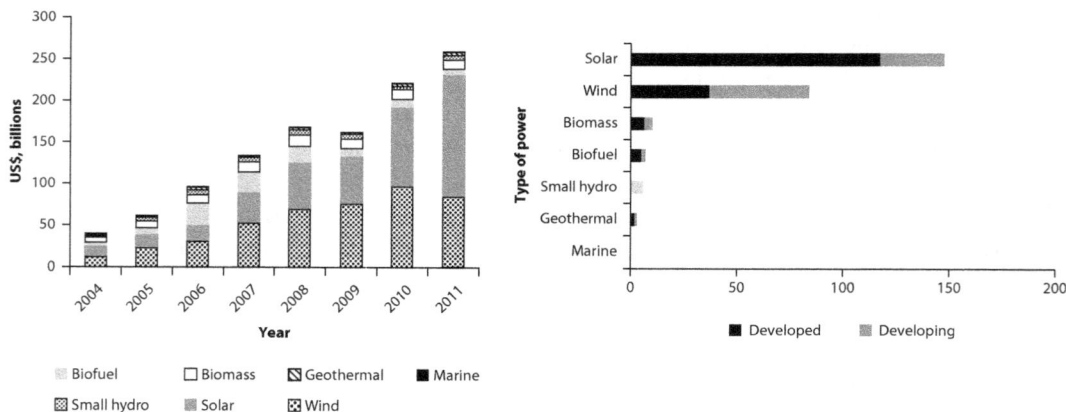

■ Developed ■ Developing

Biofuel □ Biomass ◫ Geothermal ■ Marine
▨ Small hydro ■ Solar ⊠ Wind

Source: Bloomberg New Energy Finance.

For many developing countries, investment is hampered by both the lack of financial viability for clean carbon technology packages and planning approaches that often fail to appropriately value and integrate clean carbon technologies. The menu of financing sources available to renewable energy projects depends on the maturity of the technology involved—whether it's "pre-commercialization" (like a carbon capture and storage), "not financially competitive" (like renewable electricity, such as wind), or "mature"(typically energy efficiency, such as lighting (CFLs)).

Phasing Out Energy Subsidies

For some countries, phasing out energy subsidies could become a vital source of financing for power sector improvements and climate change mitigation and adaptation activities. These subsidies, which consume billions of dollars in many countries are no longer affordable for many state governments, but removing them right now is tough politically. In Uzbekistan, energy subsidies amounted to over 30 percent of GDP in 2010 (EIA 2011; IEA, OPEC, OECD and Word Bank 2011). The most heavily subsidized item is oil, followed by natural gas and electricity. As these subsidies are phased out, countries will realize numerous benefits.

Efficiency gain. Phasing out subsidies would achieve efficiency gains by removing market distortions. Subsidies that artificially lower energy prices result in an economically inefficient allocation of resources and market distortions, encourage wasteful consumption, exacerbate energy-price volatility by blurring market signals, incentivize fuel adulteration and smuggling, and undermine the competitiveness of renewables and more efficient energy technologies (IEA 2010).

Environmental benefit. Phasing out subsidies would help climate change. Market-based instruments for mitigation include putting a price on carbon, either through a carbon tax or an emissions trading scheme. But energy subsidies essentially reward activities that produce carbon emissions.

While the EU emissions trading scheme (EU ETS) puts a price on carbon, many countries subsidize energy, including Russia, India, non-EU eastern European countries, and oil-exporting countries. But just removing these subsidies, as figure 1.11 shows, could reduce GHG emissions in some of these countries by over 30 percent by 2050, and reduce global emissions by 10 percent (IEA *et al.* 2010; OECD 2009). This would happen because in the absence of these subsidies, demand would fall, in turn, lowering the price of fossil fuels. However, the fall in emissions would be somewhat offset by an anticipated increase in emissions in developed countries, as demand rises in response to lower fossil fuel prices. The IEA (2010) estimates that removing energy subsidies would decrease CO_2 emissions by 5.8 percent or 2 gigatons (Gt) by 2020, cutting primary energy demand by 5 percent and oil demand by 4.7 million barrels per day, or one quarter of current U.S. demand.

Economic benefit. Phasing out energy subsidies would also alleviate the financial position of cash-strapped governments. For fossil-fuel importing countries, subsidies place a significant fiscal burden on state budgets. During fossil fuel price spikes and unfavorable exchange rate fluctuations, the burden can become quite large. In Indonesia, higher international oil prices and a recovery in consumption led to a peak in energy subsidies at 4.5 percent of GDP in 2008, while public capital expenditure and spending on social programs amounted to only 1.5 percent and 1.2 percent of GDP, respectively (Mourougane 2010). For fossil fuel-exporting countries, subsidies quicken resource depletion, which can reduce long-term export earnings (IEA *et al.* 2010).

Figure 1.11 Removing Energy Subsidies in Non-OECD Countries would cut GHG Emissions

% change in emissions compared to baseline

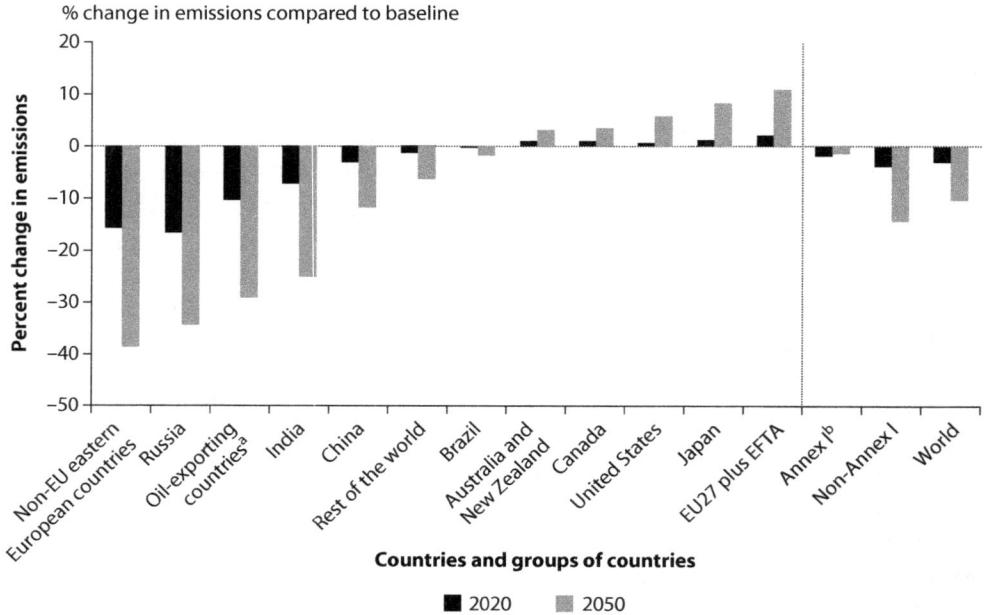

Countries and groups of countries

■ 2020   ▨ 2050

Source: OECD 2009.

Notes:

a. The region includes the Middle East, Algeria-Lybia-Egypt, Indonesia, and Venezuela.

b. Annex 1 countries are countries that have agreed to reduce their greenhouse gas emissions under the Kyoto Protocol. They include most OECD member states and some countries from Central and Eastern Europe in transition to a market economy.

The funds previously allocated for energy subsidies can instead be spent on poverty-alleviation programs. In fact, given that rates of access to basic energy services are quite low in many developing countries, energy subsidies can be regressive: funds allocated to subsidize existing consumers who can afford to pay cost-reflective prices could be better used to favor the poorest without access to energy services. Household surveys show that gasoline and transport fuel subsidies accrue mostly to the richer income quintiles.

An important condition for successful subsidy reform is the credibility of the government's commitment to compensate vulnerable groups and to use the funds freed from subsidy reform for more welfare enhancing activities. Policy tools to protect the poor include lifeline rates, which generally perform better than universal subsidies, and cash transfers. Use of transitional arrangements and short-term measures to alleviate the impact of tariff increases on the poor can act to protect low-income groups at the time of the policy change (Vagliasindi, forthcoming).

Against this backdrop of some slow down of PPP investment in the power sector in the wake of the recent financial crisis and enormous sums needed to meet the expected growing demand for power—especially in the developing world—and to cope with climate change, what is the best way to attract PPPs? Chapter 2 explores this issue, asking which incentives matter most for convincing PPPs to invest in both conventional and renewable energy sources and which incentives influence the level of investment.

References

EACC (Economics of Adaptation to Climate Change). 2009. *Economics of Adaptation to Climate Change.* Washington, DC: World Bank.

EC (European Commission). 2011. *Scaling Up International Climate Finance after 2012.* Brussels: European Commission.

EIA (Energy Information Administration). 2011. "Petroleum and Other Liquids: World Crude Oil Prices." *Energy Information Administration.* Washington, DC: US Department of Energy.

ESMAP (Energy Sector Management Assistance Program). 2010a. "East Asia Sector Assessment: Quick Assessment of the Impact of the Credit Crisis on Investments in the Power Sector." Energy Sector Management Assistance Program, World Bank, Washington, DC. http://www.esmap.org/esmap/sites/esmap.org/files/ESA_Credit_Crisis_vFINAL%20April%2014,%202009.pdf.

———. 2010b. "Impact of the Credit Crisis on Investments in the Power Sector: The Case of Egypt. Energy Sector Management Assistance Program." World Bank, Washington, DC. http://www.esmap.org/esmap/sites/esmap.org/files/Egypt_Power FinanceVulnerability(Feb2010final).pdf.

———. 2010c. "Impact of the Credit Crisis on Investments in the Power Sector: The Case of Tunisia. Energy Sector Management Assistance Program." World Bank, Washington, DC. http://www.esmap.org/esmap/sites/esmap.org/files/Esmap%20 Vulnerability%20Tunisia%2001%2012.pdf.

———. 2010d. "Impact of the Global Financial Crisis on Investments in South Asia's Electric Power Infrastructure. Energy Sector Management Assistance Program." World Bank, Washington, DC. http://www.esmap.org/esmap/sites/esmap.org/files/SA%20 FINAL%20REPORT%20PDF.pdf.

———. 2010e. "Impact of the Credit Crisis on Investments in the Power Sector: International Players and the MENA Region. Energy Sector Management Assistance Program." World Bank, Washington, DC. http://www.esmap.org/esmap/sites/esmap .org/files/Esmap%20Vulnerability%20MENA%20General%2001%2012_0.pdf.

———. 2010f. "Impact of the Credit Crisis on Investments in the Power Sector: The Case of Jordan. Energy Sector Management Assistance Program." World Bank, Washington, DC. http://www.esmap.org/esmap/sites/esmap.org/files/Jordan_PowerFinanceVulner ability(Feb2010final)_0.pdf.

Foster, V., and C. Briceño-Garmendia. 2010. *Africa's Infrastructure: A Time for Transformation. Africa Infrastructure Country Diagnostic.* Washington, DC: World Bank. http://www4.worldbank.org/afr/ssatp/Resources/HTML/Conferences/Lilong we09/proceedings/04-Foster-AICD.pdf.

IEA (International Energy Agency). 2008. *Energy Technology Perspectives.* Paris: OECD.

———. 2010. *Energy Technology Perspectives.* Paris: OELD.

———. 2011. *World Energy Outlook.* Paris: OELD.

IEA (International Energy Agency), OPEC (Organization of the Petroleum Exporting Countries), OECD (Organization for Economic Co-operation and Development), and World Bank. 2010. "Analysis of the Scope of Energy Subsidies and Suggestions for the G-20 Initiatives." Paper submitted to the G-20 Summit Meeting Toronto, June 26–27.

IPCC (Intergovernmental Panel on Climate Change). 2007. *Fourth Assessment Report Synthesis Report* Geneva, Switzerland: IPCC.

McKinsey & Company, "A Cost Curve for Greenhouse Gas Reduction,". *McKinsey Quarterly*, February 2007. http://www.mckinseyquarterly.com/A_cost_curve_for_greenhouse_gas_reduction_1911.

———. 2009. *Pathways to a Low-carbon Economy. Version 2 of the Global Greenhouse Gas Abatement Cost Curve.* McKinsey & Company. https://solutions.mckinsey.com/ClimateDesk/default.aspx.

———. 2010. *Impact of the Financial Crisis on Carbon Economics: Version 2.1 of the Global Greenhouse Gas Abatement Cost Curve.* McKinsey & Company. http://www.mckinsey.com/client_service/sustainability/latest_thinking/greenhouse_gas_abatement_cost_curves.

Mourougane, A. 2010. "Phasing Out Energy Subsidies in Indonesia." OECD Economics Department Working Papers, No. 808, OECD Publishing. http://dx.doi.org/10.1787/5km5xvc9c46k-en.

NEPAD (New Partnership for Africa's Development). 2009. *Revision of the AU/NEPAD African Action Plan 2010–2015: Advancing Regional and Continental Integration Together through Shared Values, Abridged Report 2010–2012.* Johannesburg, South Africa: NEPAD. http://www.oecd.org/dataoecd/59/20/47693615.pdf.

NEPAD-OECD (New Partnership for Africa's Development-Organization for Economic Co-operation and Development). 2009. "Increasing Private Investment in African Energy Infrastructure." Background Paper, Ministerial and Expert Roundtable for the NEPAD-OECD Africa Investment Initiative on November 11–12, 2009. Paris: OECD. http://www.oecd.org/dataoecd/44/46/43966848.pdf.

OECD (Organization for Economic Co-operation and Development). 2008. *OECD Environmental Outlook to 2030.* Paris: OECD.

———. 2009. *Cost-Effective Actions to Tackle Climate Change. Policy Brief, August 2009.* Paris: OECD.

Parry, M. 2009. *Assessing the Costs of Adaptation to Climate Change: A Review of the UNFCCC and Other Recent Estimates.* Imperial College London, UK: International Institute for Environment and Development and the Grantham Institute for Climate Change.

Project Catalyst. 2009. "Scaling up Climate Finance." Finance Briefing Paper. http://www.climateworks.org/download/Scaling-up-climate-finance.

Stern, N. 2007. *The Economics of Climate Change: The Stern Review.* London: Cabinet Office, HM Treasury.

UNFCCC (UN Framework Convention on Climate Change). 2007a. *Call for Input on Non-Binding Best-Practice Examples on the Demonstration of Additionality to Assist the Development of PDDs, Particularly for SSC Project Activities.* Bonn: UNFCCC.

———. 2007b. *Investment and Financial Flows to Address Climate Change.* Bonn: UNFCCC.

———. 2008. *Investment and Financial Flows to Address Climate Change: An Update.* Bonn: UNFCCC.

———. 2011. "CDM in Numbers." Bonn: UNFCCC. http://cdm.unfccc.int/Statistics/index.html.

Vagliasindi, M. 2012. *Implementing Energy Subsidy Reforms.* Washington, DC: World Bank, Direction in Development.

World Bank. 2009. The Impact of the Global Economic Crisis on Core Expenditures: Infrastructure Maintenance II, Sustainable Development Network Briefing Note, Washington, DC: World Bank.

———. 2010a. *Financial Crisis: Threat or Opportunity for Power Sectors of ECA Countries?* Washington, DC: World Bank.

———. 2010b. *Assessing the Impact of the Financial and Economic Crisis on Energy Sector Investment Requirements in Latin America and the Caribbean Region.* Washington, DC: World Bank.

———. 2011. "Mobilizing Climate Finance." Paper submitted to the G20 October 6, 2011. Washington, DC.

CHAPTER 2

How PPPs Are Faring Globally

The global picture for energy investment is changing—and rapidly. In 2008, for the first time, renewable energy (including large hydro) attracted more power sector investment globally than fossil-fuel based technologies, according to UNEP (2011). Moreover, renewable sources of energy are expected to triple by 2035, according to the International Energy Agency's New Policies scenario (IEA 2010). This growth is being driven by an alignment of global factors (1) a rapid rise in energy demand from emerging economies such as China and India; (2) increased competition for energy resources; (3) geopolitical tension and energy security concerns; (4) rising oil and gas prices; and (5) the entry into force of the Kyoto Protocol in early 2005, along with a higher political interest in climate change.

In recent years, global investment in renewable energy has jumped from around US$23 billion in 2004 to around US$114 billion in 2007 and following a drop after the global financial crisis, climbing back up to a peak of almost US$173 billion in 2011 (figure 2.1). If research and development programs are included global investments equal US$257 in 2011, of which 65 percent were generated from developed countries and 35 percent in developing countries.

At this point, renewable energy still represents a marginal percentage of the world's generation mix—in terms of global installed capacity, about 9 percent as of 2011 (excluding large hydropower), although up from around 5 percent in 2004 (figure 2.2). But its share in total new capacity additions (including hydropower) has grown exponentially, from 10 percent in 2004 to 44 percent in 2010.

How is this energy picture likely to evolve in terms of the level and composition of investment? The change would be drastic if a move toward low carbon solutions is implemented through an increasing proportion of renewable energy. Most renewable sources of energy cost more than energy from fossil fuels, typically because of higher upfront capital costs, although these costs are rapidly falling. Once projects have begun, operational costs are lower than for energy fossil fuels—for example, wind and solar, do not have a fuel cost or fuel price volatility to manage. Renewable energy project financing also involves longer financing structures. Before the global financial crisis,

Figure 2.1 Global Investment in Renewable Energy Has Risen Sharply

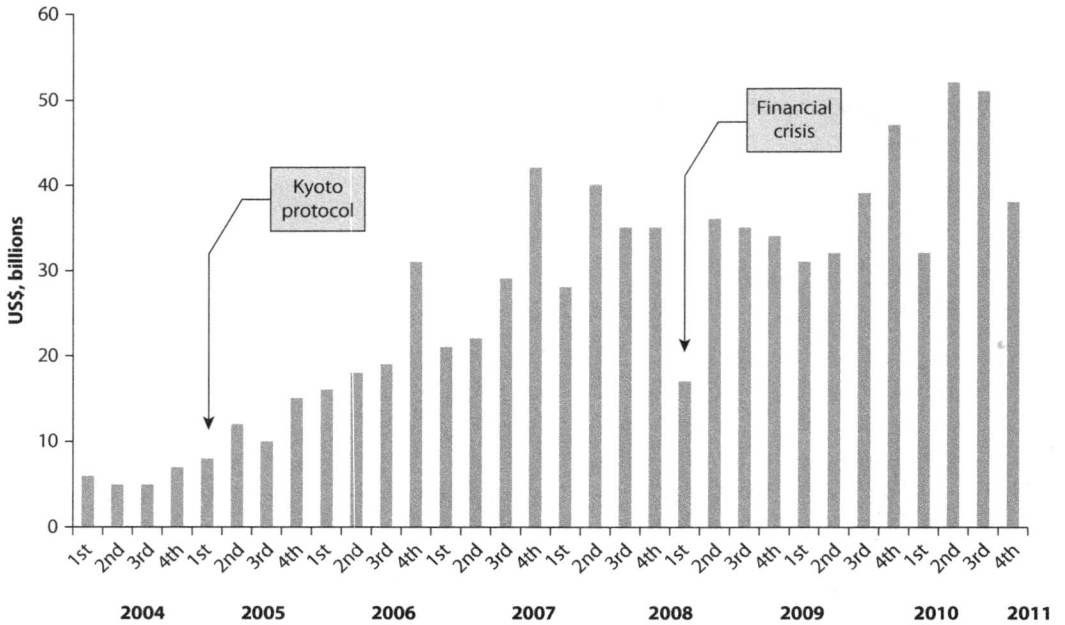

maturities extended to 15 years or more to repay upfront loans, through income stemming from the project's power generation. This makes renewable energy power projects exposed to longer term risk, including the policy and regulatory incentive environment.

Figure 2.2 Renewable Total Capacity Is Still Low, but New Capacity Is Growing Exponentially

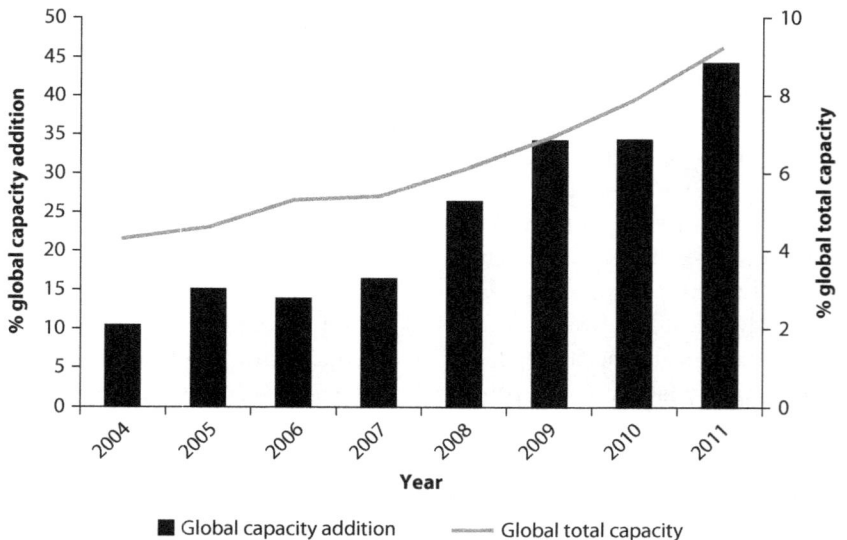

Given the higher costs and risk of renewables, companies—particularly in the private sector—are unwilling to invest unless they are required to or offered economic and financial incentives to do so (such as through price support mechanisms). This situation matters because private investors are needed to supplement public sector investment, especially given the additional daunting tab that will come from investments to cope with climate change (mitigation and adaptation). Furthermore, the biggest share of future investment will be needed in the developing world, where demand for power is expected to grow exponentially in response to development and population growth.

What is the best way to encourage public-private partnerships (PPPs) in the power sector in developing countries? To shed more light on this issue, we undertook a study to gauge which factors encourage private investment in electricity generated by fossil fuels (oil, coal, and natural gas) and renewables (hydro, wind, waste and geothermal). We used an econometric analysis, covering 105 developing countries from 1993 to 2008. We grouped these factors into three areas: sectoral and economy-wide governance, long-run environmental sustainability drivers, and short-run crises and long-term economic fundamentals.

This chapter begins with a look at how PPP investment in the power sector is changing and what we know already about the role of governance and its impact on performance. We then explain how the study was done and our key findings. The highlights are:

- Support mechanisms, like feed-in tariffs, are crucial for attracting investors in generation, but they could play a bigger role in affecting the level of investment
- Regulatory certainty is vital for attracting investors in renewables for generation, transmission, and distribution
- The implementation of the Kyoto Protocol combined with higher fuel prices is important in attracting PPPs in renewables, underscoring the value of legal commitments
- Control for corruption and degree of political competition primarily affect investors' decisions to enter the various power sector markets, not the subsequent level of investment—indicating that investors seem to be adequately protected against risks
- Market size (as measured by population) matters more than the "affordability" level of consumers (as measured by income) for attracting PPPs in the power sector.

A Profile of PPP Power Activities

So what does the latest data tell us about PPP investment in the power sector—and here we will focus on the developing world. On a regional basis, the key summary statistics show that PPP investment is highly concentrated (figure 2.3). For generation from conventional sources, East Asia and the Pacific (EAP) leads,

Figure 2.3 Most PPP Investment in the Power Sector Comes from ...

a. East Asia and Latin America Lead in Generation

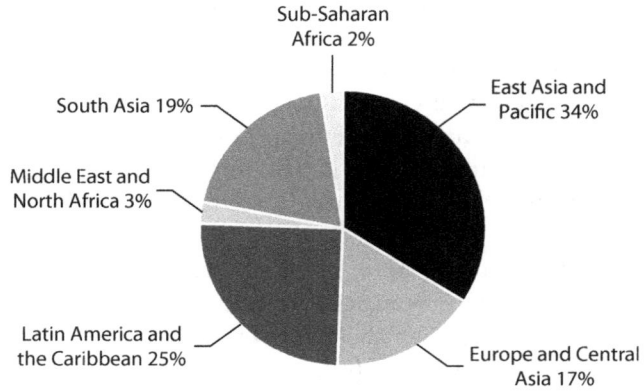

Sub-Saharan Africa 2%

South Asia 19%

Middle East and North Africa 3%

East Asia and Pacific 34%

Latin America and the Caribbean 25%

Europe and Central Asia 17%

b. Including Renewables

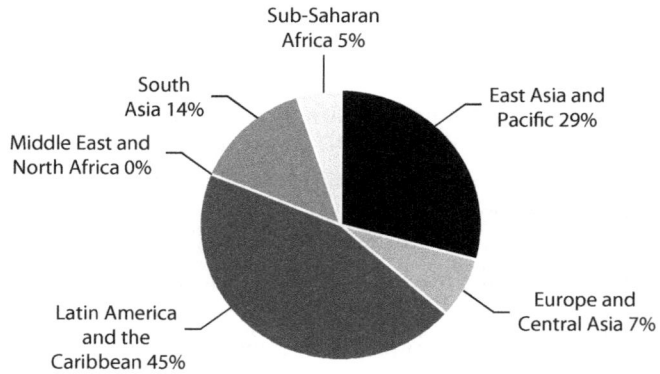

Sub-Saharan Africa 5%

South Asia 14%

Middle East and North Africa 0%

East Asia and Pacific 29%

Latin America and the Caribbean 45%

Europe and Central Asia 7%

c. and Latin America for Transmission and Distribution

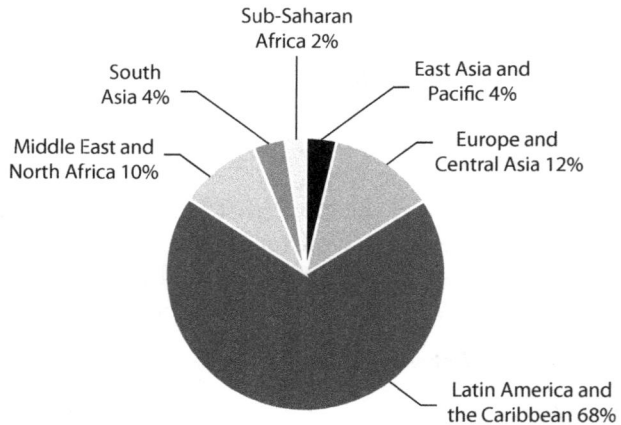

Sub-Saharan Africa 2%

South Asia 4%

Middle East and North Africa 10%

East Asia and Pacific 4%

Europe and Central Asia 12%

Latin America and the Caribbean 68%

Source: World Bank/PPIAF PPI Database.

closely followed by Latin America and the Caribbean (LAC) leads, and, with a significant gap, the South Asian Region (SAR) and Europe and Central Asia (ECA). For generation from renewable, LAC leads, closely followed by EAP, and with a gap, ECA. In the Middle East and North Africa (MNA) and Sub-Saharan Africa (SSA), little investment in generation has been recorded. In transmission and distribution, LAC leads, followed, but with a significant gap, by ECA and MNA. In the remaining regions, here, too, little investment has been recorded.

Of the total PPP investment in electricity generation, fossil fuels account for the lion's share—about 75 percent (figure 2.4). Coal accounts for 35 percent, natural gas 24 percent, and fuel oil 15 percent. Total investment in renewables represents a mere 4 percent, if hydropower, at 22 percent, is excluded. Within that group, wind and geothermal technologies have almost an equal share of about 40 percent, with waste limited to 20 percent.

Although the current share of PPP investment in renewables among developing countries is still quite small, the data show a dramatic rise in this type of investment—following the adoption of the Kyoto Protocol in 1997 and the introduction of support schemes (particularly feed-in tariffs) in Europe in the early 1990s. The East Asian and Russian crises in 1997/98, as well as the Latin American crisis in 2001, hurt PPP investments in renewables, but recent short-run shocks have taken less of a toll.

Among the fossil fuels, there is some evidence of switching of PPP investment from oil and coal to natural gas (figure 2.5). Indeed, natural gas is the only fossil fuel that has substantially increased its share of PPP investment from about 10 percent in the early 1990s to above 50 percent in 2002, then decreasing to below 40 percent in 2008—although in dollar terms, 2008 was a peak, with investment reaching above US$12 billion. There is also some evidence of switching of PPP investment from fossil fuels to hydro and renewables.

Figure 2.4 PPP Investment in Renewables is Still Small and Mostly in Wind and Geothermal

a. Coal, Oil, Nature Gas, Hydro, and Renewables   **b. Geothermal, Waste, Wind, and Solar**

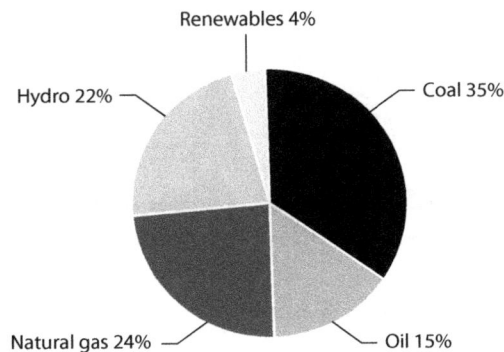

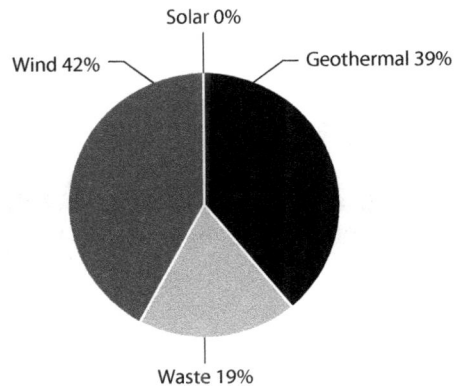

Source: World Bank/PPIAF PPI Database.

Figure 2.5 PPP Investment in Natural Gas, Hydro, and Wind is Growing
by energy source, US$ million

a. Renewable, Hydro, Natural Gas, Oil, and Coal   **b. Solar, Wind, Waste, and Geothermal**

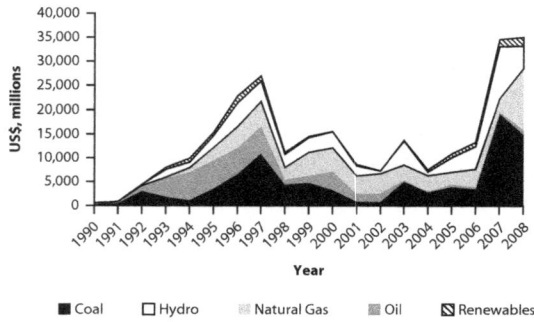
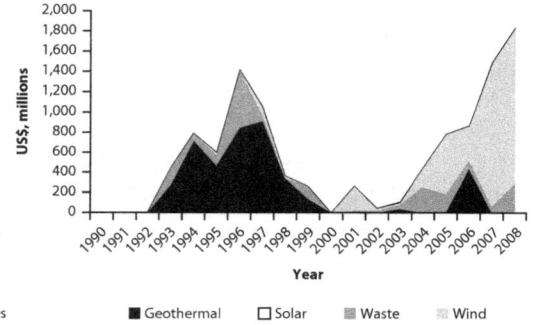

■ Coal   □ Hydro   ▨ Natural Gas   ▨ Oil   ◩ Renewables   ■ Geothermal   □ Solar   ▨ Waste   ▨ Wind

Source: World Bank/PPIAF PPI Database.

Not surprisingly, each region has attracted PPP investment based on its energy endowment and untapped potential (figure 2.6).

- East Asia leads in attracting the most oil and coal (more than 40 percent), geothermal (more than 80 percent), waste (70 percent), and wind (just below 50 percent)
- Latin America leads in attracting the most natural gas (35 percent) and renewable, including hydropower (50 percent)

Figure 2.6 Global PPP Investment in Various Energy Sources
1990–2008, US$ million

a. Coal   **b. Oil**

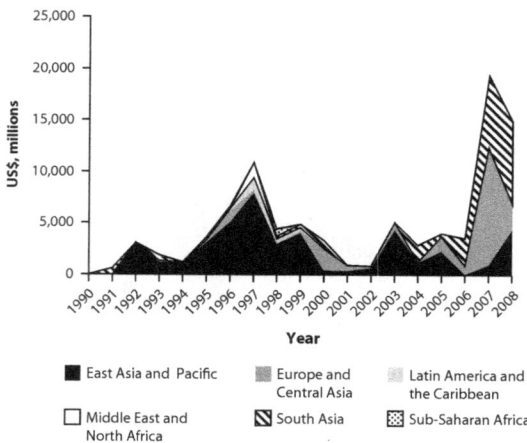
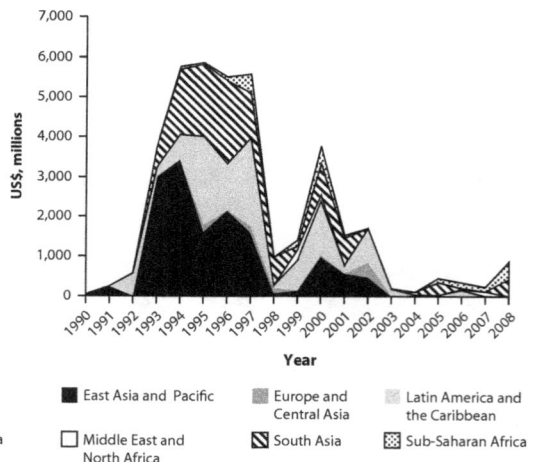

■ East Asia and Pacific   ▨ Europe and Central Asia   ▨ Latin America and the Caribbean   ■ East Asia and Pacific   ▨ Europe and Central Asia   ▨ Latin America and the Caribbean

□ Middle East and North Africa   ◩ South Asia   ▨ Sub-Saharan Africa   □ Middle East and North Africa   ◩ South Asia   ▨ Sub-Saharan Africa

(figure continues on next page)

Figure 2.6 Global PPP Investment in Various Energy Sources (*continued*)

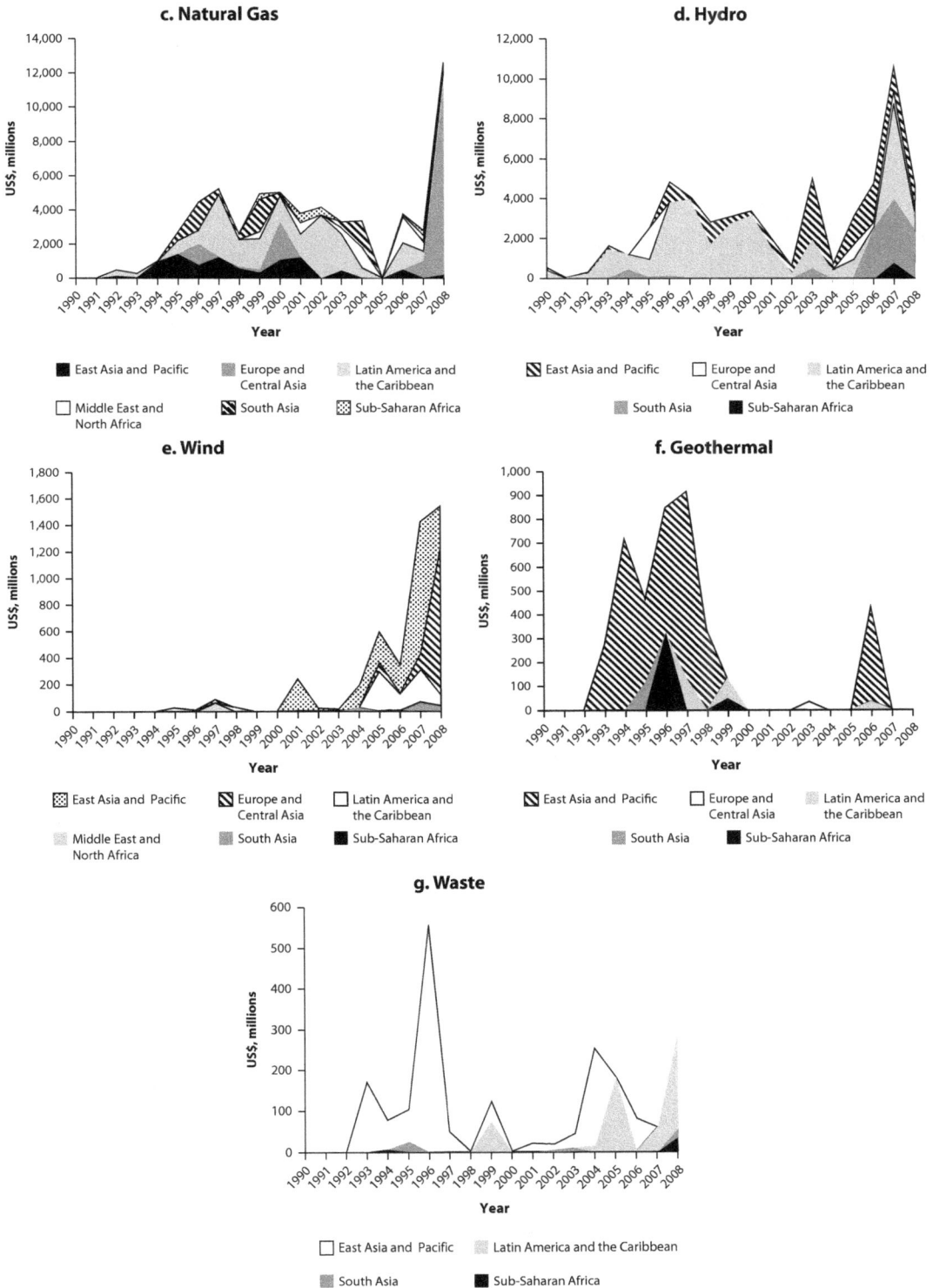

c. Natural Gas

d. Hydro

e. Wind

f. Geothermal

g. Waste

Source: World Bank/PPIAF PPI Database.

- South Asia is second in attracting oil and coal (more than 40 percent), and it experienced the biggest growth in hydropower (for a total of just below 20 percent)
- ECA is second in attracting natural gas (about 30 percent), and it experienced the most impressive exponential growth in wind (for a total of about 30 percent).

Coal. PPP investment in coal-based generation reached its first peak of US$10 billion in 1997, then declined sharply after the East Asian crisis, but rose to a new peak of US$20 billion in 2007. EAP accounts for the largest share of cumulated private investment in coal (about 50 percent of the total investment in this fuel), followed by SAR and ECA. The other three regions account for very small percentages.

Oil. PPP investment in oil-based generation declined sharply from the peak of US$6 billion in 1995 to US$100 million in 2004, but edged up again in recent years, reaching alm ost US$900 million in 2008, triggered by the emergency rental of diesel mobile plants to face power outages. EAP accounts for the largest share of total cumulated investment in oil, although the share has declined sharply from 80 percent in 1993 to 5 percent in 2005 and zero since 2006. LAC's share has also declined sharply from almost 100 percent in 1992 to 40 percent in 2006 and then zero. However, two regions have been boosting their shares. SAR has increased its share from an insignificant percentage in the early 1990s to more than 70 percent in 1998, and is now about 50 percent. SSA is the region for which oil-based generation has increased the most, given its vulnerability to severe power outages, which require emergency intervention.

Natural Gas. PPP investment in natural gas-based generation first peaked at above US$5 billion in 1997, then declined sharply after the East Asian crisis and stabilized at levels above US$4,000, only to shoot up to a new peak of US$12 billion in 2008. This recent investment boom was driven by ECA, which accounted for almost 90 percent of the total annual investment. LAC accounts for the largest share of total cumulated private investment in natural gas, although its annual share has declined sharply from 80 percent in 1993 to 40 percent in 2006 to 5 percent in 2008. EAP has the second largest share of total cumulated investment, but most of the new investment took place up to 2001 and has since declined sharply. Besides ECA, new investment is picking up in SAR, which accounts for about 15 percent of the cumulated investment and, since 2004, 45 percent of the annual investment. A similar rising trend is occurring in MENA, which accounts for about 10 percent of the cumulated investment but, as of 2006, 40 percent of the annual investment.

Hydropower. PPP investment in hydropower first peaked at slightly above US$4 billion in the mid-1990s and then again in 2003, before falling off and then shooting up to over US$10 billion in 2007. LAC is the big driver, with Brazil alone attracting more than 35 percent of the PPP hydropower investment in developing countries, followed by Chile and Argentina each with more than 5 percent of investment. The other big player is South Asia, with India accounting for more than 15 percent of investment and China about 10 percent.

Specific risks for hydropower investment arise for project financing, such as hydrological uncertainty, construction cost overruns, schedule slippage, and power demand uncertainty.

Geothermal. PPP investment in geothermal first peaked at US$720 million in 1994, then US$920 million in 1997 before falling down to a peak of US$400 million in 2006. EAP hosts some of the largest resources of geothermal energy in the world, with both Indonesia and the Philippines announcing intentions to become the world leader in geothermal production. Indonesia alone accounts for 40 percent of global geothermal potential, and it is leading with 40 percent of total investment, followed by the Philippines with 33 percent. In SSA, geothermal is a key resource for countries along the East African Rift Valley System, such as the Democratic Republic of Congo and Kenya. In Central America, El Salvador is the largest producer of geothermal energy, followed by Costa Rica and Guatemala.

Investment in geothermal has significant upfront costs that must be spent prior to determining the viability of the resource basin. Key variables are (1) the short-term, up-front geological risk of exploration drilling and (2) the long-term geological risk of developing and producing a geothermal reservoir with a lower than estimated temperature, higher than estimated mineralization, or difficulty with injection of geothermal fluids back into the subsurface.

Wind. PPP investment in wind reached US$240 million in 2001, then US$600 million in 2005 and then close to US$1.6 billion in 2008. China alone attracted more than 50 percent of PPP investment in wind. Not surprisingly, China is listed as the top country in the world in terms of wind power added capacity in 2009, ahead of the United States, Spain, Germany, and India and the second country after the United States in terms of existing capacity. Poland has been a fast mover, attracting 15 percent of the overall investment since 2005. Bulgaria follows, with more than 8 percent. It is also worth noting the effort by Turkey and India in attracting private investment in wind, which accounts for about 3 percent of the total PPP investment in each of the countries.

The risk of lower revenue from a wind project owing to lower than expected wind speeds is a major factor affecting the finance terms and conditions of wind farms. For wind as for other grid-connected renewable-based energy, long lead times and an administrative process may be needed to ensure grid reinforcements or additional investment necessary in the distribution or transmission system. Regulations requiring the project developer to pay the grid cost only up to the nearest grid connection point (the so called "shallow" grid connection charges) minimize the risks for the project developers, but they increase the burden on the network operator.

Waste. PPP investment in waste reached its high at about US$560 million in 1996, fell sharply after the Asian crisis, and is now close US$300 million. Thailand alone accounts for 50 percent of the total PPP waste investment in developing countries, with biomass by far the largest contributor to power generation and the second largest source of renewable energy. Other countries notably active in this area are Brazil with more than 20 percent of the total PPP waste investment, and China with 12 percent. Municipal solid waste projects have been proposed but only infrequently implemented. Privately owned renewable energy projects that produce electricity under the Small Power Producer (SPP) and Very Small Power Producers have been pioneered in Thailand and Sri Lanka and, recently in SSA with Tanzania (box 2.1).

Box 2.1

Small Power Producers and "Light Handed Regulation"

Small Power Producer (SPP) regulations enable expansion of renewable generated electricity through model power purchase agreements, standardized tariffs, and streamlined interconnection and licensing requirements. The regulations provide the legal basis for customers to self-supply with small clean renewable energy or cogeneration generators and to export excess power (up to 10 megawatts) to the national utility (either the national grid or mini-grids).

But SPPs will only develop if the prices that they receive for their electrical output exceed their own costs of production. For example, where main grid connected SPPs can sell at an administratively set price of about US$10 per kilowatt-hour, the only SPPs that are commercially viable are cogenerators, some biomass generators, and some mini-hydro generators with well-endowed sites. Solar and wind generators are generally not viable at this price level.

In Tanzania, SPPs will occasionally replace some or all of the production of existing diesel generation of mini-grids operated by TANESCO (the national government-owned utility). In other cases, it will bring electricity to communities without electricity. EWURA, the Tanzanian electricity regulator, has made a conscious effort to employ "light handed regulation" in its regulation of SPPs. This means (1) minimizing the amount of information that is required, (2) minimizing the number of different regulatory requirements and decisions, and (3) relying to the extent possible on related reviews by other Tanzanian government entities.

Both Thailand and Sri Lanka, with similar SPP regulations, have encountered problems in which companies apply for PPAs with the intention of selling these PPAs at a profit. In Thailand, one company accounts for 445 megawatts of signed PPAs for grid-connected solar photovoltaic (PV), but none of these projects have been built. In Sri Lanka, companies have tied up key micro-hydro sites with PPAs that have failed to develop into projects even after a number of years. To discourage this form of "PPA speculation," EWURA's license approvals "expire" after two years, giving other developers the chance to move in and develop the site.

Sources: Greacen *et al.* 2010; Tenenbaum and Greacen 2010.

As for transmission and distribution, the past financial crises—notably the East Asian and Russian crisis in 1997/98 as well as the Latin American crisis in 2001—have hurt PPP investment (figure 2.7). In distribution, most of the privatizations in Latin America took place in the 1990s, with investment peaking at about US$14 billion in 1997 (accounting for about 80 percent of the total global PPP investment in distribution that year). Eastern Europe and Central Asia followed with investment peaking at about US$1.4 billion in 2005 (accounting for about 80 percent of the total global PPP investment in distribution that year).

In transmission, most LAC private sector participation took place in the second half of 2000, with a peak of about US$2.5 billion in 2006 (accounting for more than 95 percent of the total global PPP investment in transmission that year). In SAR, which came in second, investment peaked at about US$700 million in 2007 (accounting for about 80 percent of the total global PPP investment in transmission that year). In ECA, a few countries, including Romania and Georgia, have attracted private investment with considerable success. Transelectrica SA, the Romanian transmission operator, was the first state-owned company listed on the Bucharest Stock Exchange in 2006, recording significant improvement in technical and financial performance (box 2.2). In Georgia, the Irish company ESBI was awarded a five-year management contract to improve performance of the Georgian State Electrosystem, the Georgian state owned transmission operator, in 2003. The contract represents one of the few cases—and a successful one—of the use of management contracts in transmission (box 2.3).

Figure 2.7 Asian Crisis Took a Major Toll on PPP Investment in Distribution
by region over time, US$ million

a. Distribution Only

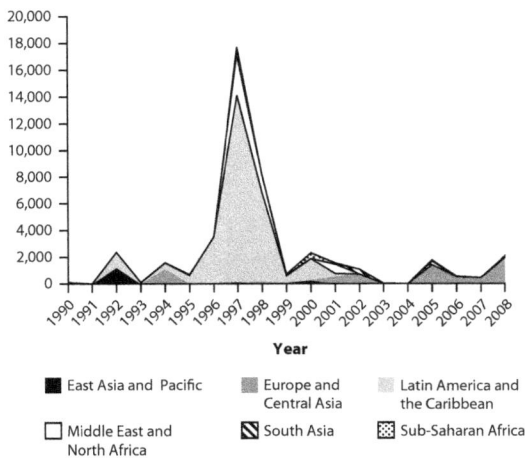

b. Transmission Only

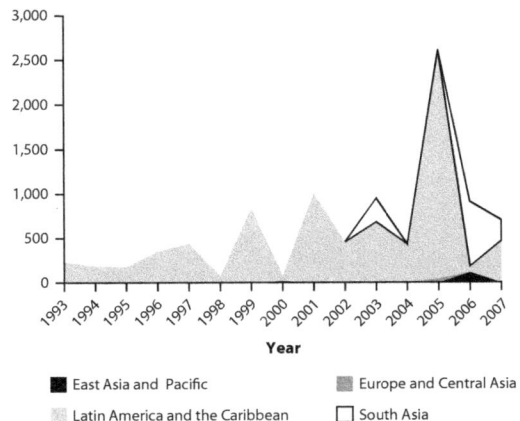

Legend for a. Distribution Only:
- East Asia and Pacific
- Europe and Central Asia
- Latin America and the Caribbean
- Middle East and North Africa
- South Asia
- Sub-Saharan Africa

Legend for b. Transmission Only:
- East Asia and Pacific
- Europe and Central Asia
- Latin America and the Caribbean
- South Asia

Source: World Bank/PPIAF PPI Database.

Box 2.2

Public Listing of Romania's Transmission Operator

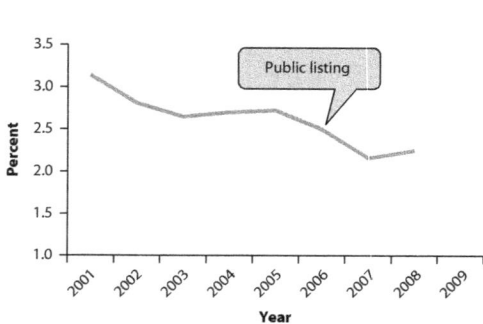

Transelectrica SA, the Romanian transmission operator, was the first state-owned company to be listed on the Bucharest Stock Exchange, with 10 percent of its shares listed at the end of August 2006. This followed the company's successful 2001 restructuring. Although the number of employees stayed about the same, labor productivity (measured as revenues per employee) rose sharply from before the restructuring, reaching peak levels in 2006 and the following years. On the financial side, the company experienced losses in 2002/03 but then turned profitable and remained so—hitting a high the year of the listing—although profits fell off in 2009 following the financial crisis.

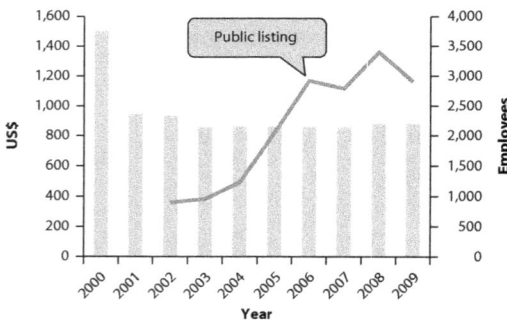

In terms of transmission losses and failure, the company already had a low level before the public listing, thanks to the restructuring, and further improvement occurred after the listing.

Figure B2.2a Productivity and Profitability Improved after the Restructuring and Listing

a. Revenues per Employee   **b. Operational profit and dividend**

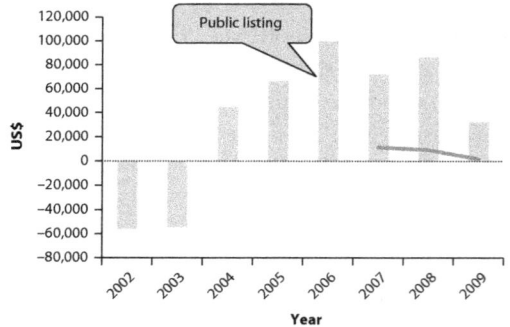

Figure B2.2b Transmission Losses and Failures also Got Better

a. Transmission Losses   **b. Transmission Failures**

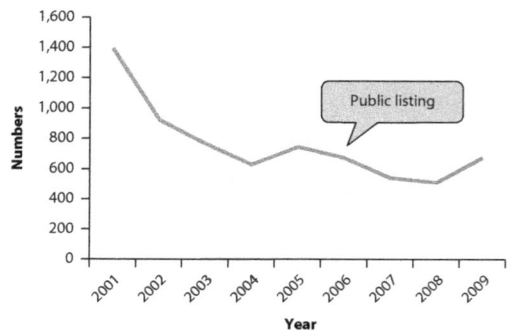

Source: Transelectrica (various years) Annual Report.

Box 2.3

A Management Contract for the Georgian State Electrosystem

In 2003, Georgia gave the Irish company ESBI a five-year management contract to overhaul the Georgian State Electrosystem, which had been experiencing major financial and operational problems. The result was a dramatic improvement in the the state-owned transmission operator's performance.

On the financial side, the number of employees was reduced sharply from 4,500 employees in 2002 to 1,048 in 2007 (the last year of the contract), enabling an almost threefold rise in labor productivity. Profitability also increased, as the cash collection rate jumped from 36 percent in 2003 to about 100 percent in 2007. In fact, the utility managed to post a profit in 2005, after reporting losses for a number of years before, and remained profitable (although there was a significant 2006 dip) until 2009, after the contract's end.

Figure B2.3a Productivity and Profitability Has Improved

a. Revenue per Employee

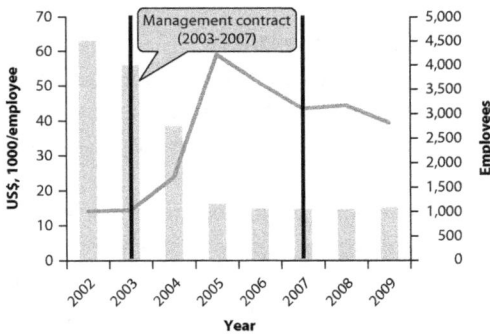

b. Profit/Loss

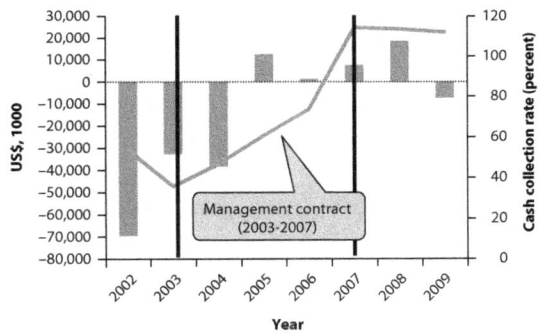

Source: World Bank data.

Figure B2.3b Transmission Losses and Blackouts Have Plummeted

a. Transmission Losses

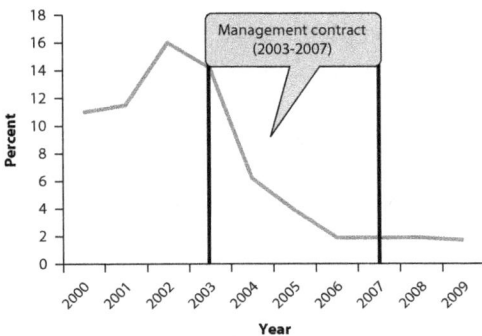

b. Black Outs

Blackout   Partial blackouts

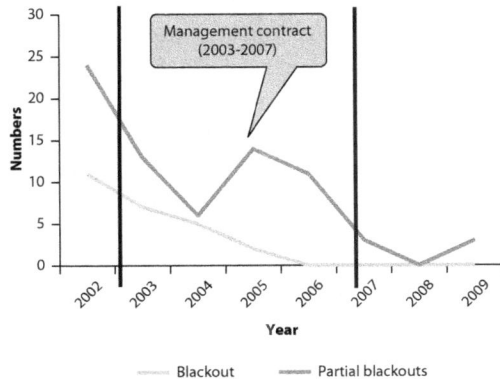

Source: Econ Poyry 2008. The electricity sector in Georgia A risk assessment and Georgian State Electrosystem (Several Years) Annual Report.

(box continues on next page)

Box 2.3 A Management Contract for the Georgian State Electrosystem *(continued)*

Another challenge faced by the ESBI management team was a high level of transmission losses, which had reached 16 percent of the purchased electricity by 2003. But by 2006, these were lowered to about 2 percent—a level comparable to West European transmission systems losses—and have stayed there. The high level of blackouts was also ended, falling from 11 in 2002 to zero in 2006, and staying there. The number of partial blackouts also dropped significantly, from 24 in 2003 to under 5 by 2007, and they have remained low.

The Role of Sectoral Governance

What has been the biggest hurdle for developing countries in attracting investment in renewable? The prevailing belief in policy circles and the literature is that sectoral governance issues matter greatly—notably, support mechanisms and regulation.

The Role of Renewable Support Mechanisms in Generation

Renewable energy support and incentive mechanisms are the key factors driving the growth of a market in renewables. Current policies that support renewable energy use either price—the most popular one—or quantity setting instruments, although they can be used together.

Price-based systems. The main price-based system is feed-in tariffs, which obligate electric utilities to purchase renewable energy through long-term contracts that guarantee access to the grid at a guaranteed price or an addition to the prevailing market price. They are attractive because a stable revenue stream across a pre-established timeframe reduces risk around cash-flow. Indeed, an IEA analysis indicates that the cost of capital will be higher in support schemes with traded obligations given the lack of certainty over the revenue stream.[1] These tariffs can be applied consistently and transparently and can be readily adapted to different specific power market structures—such as being offered as a premium on top of the spot-market electricity price (Cory *et al.* 2009; Couture *et al.* 2010). And they have a clear track record of delivering significant volume increases in its deployment.

Of the different options available to attract private investment in renewable energy, feed-in tariffs are increasingly seen as the "policy of choice"(Burer and Wustenhagen 2009; DB Climate Change Advisors 2010; Lesser and Su 2008; Lipp 2007; Menanteau *et al.* 2003; Mitchell *et al.* 2006; REN 21 2011). They are used in a majority of European countries, where their effectiveness has been well documented. A study comparing the effect of feed-in tariffs to other policy mechanisms designed to support the spread of wind energy found that they resulted in 7–8 times as much installed wind capacity. (European Commission, as reported by Thomas B. Johansson, Chair, Global Energy Assessment). Indeed, the overall success of the German, Spanish, Danish, and other national level feed-in programs has inspired similar initiatives in developing countries, including China and, more recently, South Africa and India, as well as regional and state governments in the United Kingdom, United States, and Australia. Globally, feed-in tariffs are current used in about 80 states and countries, more than half of which are developing economies (figure 2.8).

The most important element of feed-in tariffs is that they fully or partially remove the market risks of a project during a fixed period of time. The longer this period of guaranteed prices, the lower the cost of capital. Because of this, they are generally financed with a relatively large proportion of debt. In feed-in premium schemes, the risk of variations in electricity market prices is reflected by the tariff premium in the purchase power agreement (PPA). But private investors may struggle to acquire a PPA with a 15–20-year tenor at reasonable risk premium levels, which is why a strong government commitment toward the scheme is essential. Changes in the scheme—such as increasing the economic lifetime, the contract period in the PPA, and the debt maturity—will reduce debt service costs, but they must be done carefully to avoid seriously affecting the continuity of existing projects. This could be achieved by setting favorable conditions in loan guarantees, (low-interest) government loans, and government participation. The government can also force parties to offer long-term contracts.

A major challenge with this price-based instrument is striking the right level of feed-in tariff. A low feed-in tariff may not trigger enough investment in renewable-based energy, but a high feed-in tariff may inhibit cost reductions.

Figure 2.8 Feed-in Tariffs Are Being Increasingly Adopted Worldwide

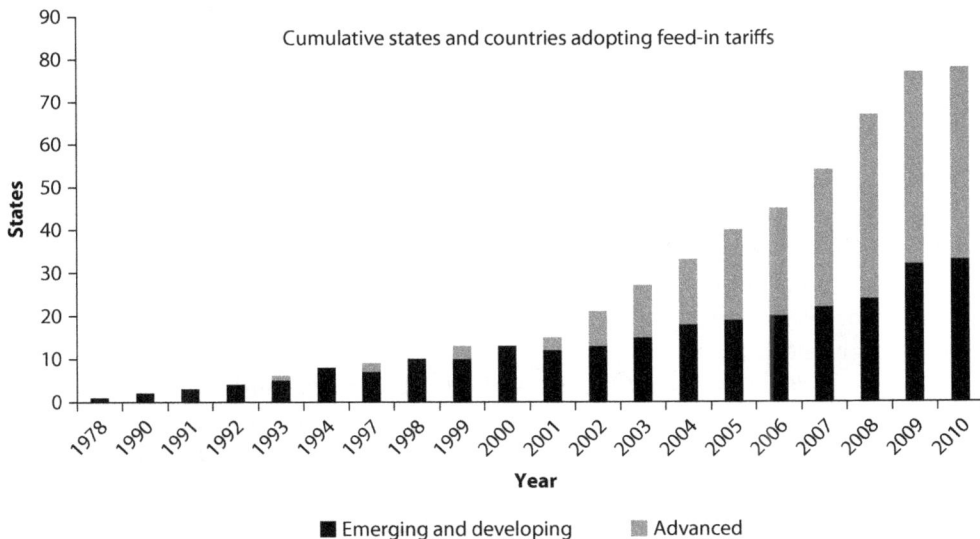

Source: REN21 2011.

This illustrates the importance of designing an efficient energy support system, which not only promotes diffusion but also provides continuous incentives for cost-reducing innovations. The rapid expansion of the Spanish solar PV and subsequent intervention to contract the market in 2008 (capping overall market size, alongside a 30 percent cut in the tariff) has been attributed as much to tariff design as to setting the tariffs at unsustainably high levels. In contrast, Germany prescribed stepped tariff reductions (degressions) and has produced steadier growth.

Quantity-based systems. A major alternative to feed-in tariffs is the system of tradable certificates or the quota obligation framework. The most popular type are renewable portfolio standards, which require utilities to supply a certain percentage from renewable energy by a given year and leave it to the market to determine the price. They are widely used in the United States, especially in developing extensive wind resources, but only a few European and developing countries have used them (box 2.4).

One problem with quotas systems is that it is more difficult to lower risk premiums in the cost of capital than with feed-in tariffs. Another problem, which has been pointed out in the U.S. experience, is that they may be less effective for incentivizing nascent, higher-cost technologies or a stable investment environment for renewables.

Even though feed-in tariff schemes and renewable portfolio standards approaches are presented as alternatives (Mitchell *et al.* 2006; Rickerson and Grace 2007), these policies can also be used together with renewable portfolio standards prescribing how much customer demand must be met with renewable-based energy and feed-in tariff policies setting the right price and providing investor certainty (Cory *et al.* 2009).

The Role of Regulatory Governance in Transmission and Distribution

The main aim of electricity regulation is to provide utilities with incentives to improve their operating and investment efficiency and to ensure that consumers benefit from the gains. Electricity distribution networks are highly capital intensive systems and timely investments to maintain and upgrade the assets are crucial for long-term reliability and expansion of their service, as well as to cope with integrating renewables. The regulators are in a position to decide what is a reasonable level of capital expenditure, a reasonable level of operating expenditure, and the allowed rate of return on regulated assets. These three elements represent around one-third each of the total regulated revenue for distribution.

In recent years, in the hopes of attracting significantly higher private investment or private finance within the public sector, major regulatory reforms have taken place in the developing world. Some efforts, such as in India and China, have been aimed at creating an effective regulatory framework. Other efforts have involved promoting independent regulatory agencies in electricity. In fact, since 1995, there has been an exponential growth in the number of autonomous

Box 2.4

Poland Uses Quota Systems for Renewable Generation

A major alternative to feed-in tariffs is the system of tradable certificates or the quota obliga-tion framework, which is a quantity based system. It has been adopted by Latvia, Poland, and Romania, and the Czech Republic (which also uses the feed-in tariff).

In 2000, the Polish government introduced a power purchase obligation for renewable energy sources, which was first amended in 2003, and again in August 2008. It requires energy suppliers to provide a certain minimum share of power generated by renewable sources (from 3.1 percent in 2005 up to 10.4 percent in 2010 and 12.9 percent in 2017). The electricity from renewable energy sources is purchased at a guaranteed price which is the median electricity price for the previous year. In 2010 this stood at 197.21 Polish Zloty (PLN) per megawatt-hour.

If a company does not fulfill its obligation according to the quota regulation, a penalty will apply that is equal to 248.46 PLN per megawatt-hour and an additional 30 percent fine cumulates to the initial fee if it is not duly paid. But the European Commission's 2007 report found that fines were not enforced. In 2005, the Polish Law on Energy (1997) was amended to obligate all renewable energy producers, regardless of the size of the instal-lations, to obtain a license from the Energy Regulation Authority. Following this new requirement, more than 600 producers of renewable energy applied for and received licenses for producing electricity from renewable sources. Since then, cumulative power installation in renewable energy has shot up from about 1,227 megawatts in 2005 to close to about 2,282 in 2010 (see table B2.4 on next page)—with wind generation taking the lead at about 1,000 megawatts in 2010 (see figure B2.4 below).

Figure B2.4 Poland's Use of Wind Power Has Skyrocketed

cumulative power installation in wind generation, MW

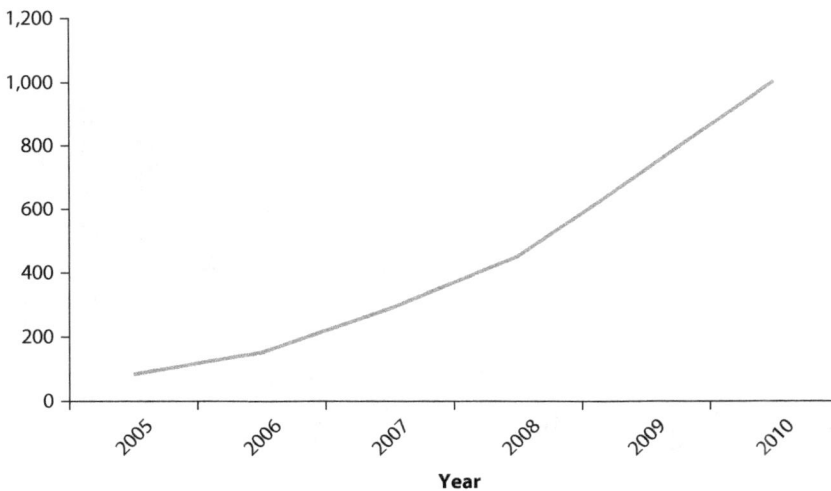

(box continues on next page)

Box 2.4 Poland Uses Quota Systems for Renewable Generation *(continued)*

Table B2.4 Hydro Comes in Second after Wind

Power source (in MW)	2005	2006	2007	2008	2009	2010
Biogas	32.00	36.80	45.70	54.61	71.62	77.00
Biomass	189.80	238.80	255.40	232.00	252.49	252.49
Wind	83.30	152.00	287.90	451.00	724.68	1,005.00
Hydro	922.00	931.00	934.80	940.57	945.20	947.00
Total	1,227.10	1,358.60	1,523.80	1,678.18	1,993.99	2,281.49

Source: Poland Energy Regulatory Office (various years) Annual Reports.

regulators in developing countries, jumping from less than 10 to about 60 in 2008 (figure 2.9).

However, despite progress in economic regulation of networks in recent years, devising suitable incentives for network investments still remains a work in progress and a challenge for many regulators (see Joskow 2008; OFGEM 2010).

On the positive side, the introduction of regulation, particularly incentive regulation regimes based on price cap regulation (RPI-X). models and bench-marking, has typically improved the efficiency of network utilities.[2] In addition, there is now more systematic evidence that better regulatory governance increases efficiency. Many recent studies—which include countries in Latin American, Asia, and Africa—show that having a regulatory agency helps (either directly or indirectly) boost mainline capacity per capita and labor productivity (such as

Figure 2.9 A Rising Number of Autonomous Regulators in Developing Countries

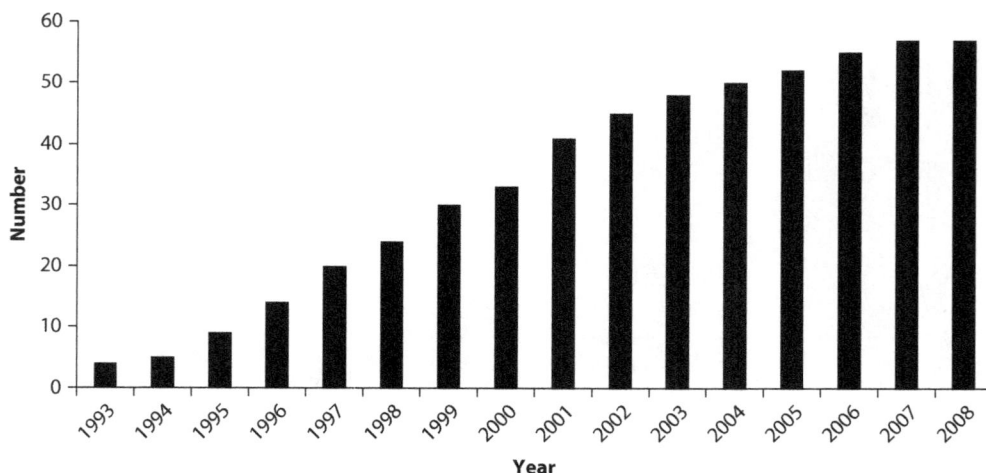

Source: World Bank data elaboration.

Cubbin and Stern 2006). Moreover, Andres *et al.* (2008) suggest that the mere existence of a regulatory agency, regardless of the utilities' ownership, significantly improves performance.

Going forward, substantial new investment in transmission and distribution networks may be needed to handle the introduction of large amounts of (both large and small scale) renewables and gas-fired microgeneration into the electricity system. Elders *et al.* (2006) identify the following technologies as being potentially important to do this: new power electronics, flexible alternating current (AC) transmission system, storage facilities, and superconducting lines. Future networks will necessitate more active management, given the intermittency of renewable energy. And the uncertainty of the timing, volume, and location of new renewables will make planning network development more difficult than before, which will also complicate regulation.

How the Econometric Study Was Done

Against this background, our study aims to identify the key factors affecting the private investor's decision to enter the market of generation, transmission, and distribution and the amount of investment sunk in each market segment. To do this, we undertook an econometric study of 105 developing countries, covering all the regions, from 1993 to 2008 (see appendix C for detailed methodology)

We divided the determinants of PPPs that are used as explanatory variables in our model into three channels (1) sectoral and economy-wide governance, (2) long-run environmental sustainability factors, and (3) short-run financial crises and economic fundamentals (see appendix C's table C.1 for dependent variables and table C.2 for explanatory variables). In these three areas, we asked the following questions:

Sectoral and Economy-wide Governance

- To what extent have support mechanisms, including feed-in tariffs, been effective in attracting private investment in renewables and encouraging some degree of switching between investment in fossil fuels and renewable-based generation?
- To what extent has higher regulatory governance been effective in attracting private investors to provide investment in transmission and distribution?
- To what extent have broader governance variables—such as control for corruption and more political competition—made a difference, vis-à-vis sectoral mechanisms in attracting private investment in each of market segments?

Long-run Environmental Sustainability Drivers

- To what extent did higher oil prices encourage a degree of switching between investment in fossil fuel and renewable-based electricity generation?
- To what extent have developing countries been able to attract and retain PPP investment, particularly in renewable energy, in the years following the

entry into force of the Kyoto Protocol, as climate change moved up the political agenda?

- To what extent have countries that prepared to integrate renewables in their systems by enhancing investment in the transmission grid, attracted higher investment in renewable-based generation?

Short-run Crises and Economic Fundamentals

- Did countries facing severe financial crises encounter problems attracting new PPPs in the power sector and then keeping that level of PPP investment after the crisis?
- What has been the influence of higher income and the size of the market on attracting PPPs and a higher volume of PPP investment?

The micro, project-level data come from the Private Participation in Infrastructure (PPI)[3] database, which is managed by the World Bank and the Private-Public Infrastructure Advisory Facility (PPIAF). The information for each project recorded in the database is (1) country and region[4]; (2) year of financial closure and total life period of the project; (3) total investment (in both monetary value and physical capacity); and (4) sector, subsector, segment, and technology (fuel) of each project.[5] The macro data are collected from other central databases, including (1) the *World Development Indicators (WDI) 2009* and the *World Governance Indicators* and Polity IV; (2) the IEA's *Energy Balances and Statistics 2009*; and (3) the U.S. Energy Information Agency.

Econometric Results

Our study shows that overall PPPs weigh governance, economic fundamentals, and climate change before even entering the power sector. As for the *level* of investment, however, governance is not a factor but economic fundamentals and climate change are (tables 2.1 and 2.2). The breakdown by generation, transmission, and distribution follows. More technical details of the econometric results are provided by Vagliasindi (2012a, 2012b, 2012c).

Generation

The results show some evidence of switching from investment in fossil fuels to investment in hydro and renewables and within fossil fuels from oil to natural gas. Such a switching decreased PPP investment in oil-based power generation. They also show the crucial importance of support schemes to attract private investment in generation (including both conventional and renewable sources).
The key results are:

- ***Sectoral governance support schemes—such as feed-in tariffs—are crucial for encouraging investment in renewable-based generation***. However, they do

Table 2.1 Before Entering the Power Market, PPPs Weigh Governance, Economic Fundamentals, and Climate Change

key determinants of introduction of PPP investment in power sector

	GEN	REN	T&D	T	D
Sectoral governance variables					
Introduction of feed-in tariffs	+**	+**	—	—	—
Electricity regulation	—	—	+***	+**	+*
Economy-wide governance variables					
Control of corruption	+***	+**	—	—	—
Degree of democracy	+**	+*	—	+**	+**
Long-run economic fundamentals					
GDP	+***	—	+***	+***	+***
Population	+***	+***	+***	+***	+***
Long-run environmental sustainability factors					
PPP investment in transmission	+**	++**	—	—	—
PPP investment in renewables	—	—	+***	+***	+***
Price of oil	−**	—	—	—	—
Price of oil*Kyoto protocol	+**	+*	—	—	—

Note: *, **, *** indicate significance of the coefficient, respectively, at 10 percent, 5 percent, and 1 percent confidence level; — = variables not included in the regression.

Table 2.2 Governance does not Affect the *level* of PPP Investment, Which Is Largely Driven by Economic Fundamentals and Climate Change

key determinants of the level of PPP investments

	GEN	REN	FF	T&D
Sectoral governance variables				
Introduction of feed-in tariffs	—	+*	—	—
Regulation	—	—	—	—
Economy-wide governance variables				
Control of corruption	—	—	—	—
Degree of democracy	—	—	—	—
Long-run economic fundamentals				
GDP	+***	+***	+***	+***
Population	+**	+**	+***	+*
Long-run environmental sustainability factors				
PPP investment in transmission	—	+***	—	—
PPP investment in renewables	—	—	—	+***
Price of oil	—	+*	—	—
Price of oil*Kyoto protocol	—	+***	—	—

Note: *, **, *** indicate significanceof the coefficient, respectively, at 10 percent, 5 percent, and 1 percent confidence level; — = variables not included in the regression.

not boost the level of investment in renewables or reduce investment in fossil fuels or drive any significant switching from fossil fuels to renewables

- *Economy-wide governance factors—such as control for corruption and degree of political competition—only affect private investors' decision to*

enter the generation market, not what happens afterwards. This suggests that
the first generations of independent power producers responded to quite favorable and long-term power purchase agreements, which shifted most of the risks
to the public sector. These mechanisms were demanded by the investors to
offset reform difficulties. For example, postponing tariff adjustments and delay-
ing unbundling efforts to separate transmission from generation reduced the
creditworthiness of power purchasers
- *Oil price increases (which correlate highly with other fossil fuel prices) drive
  investments in renewables up and those in fossil fuels down.* But because the
  reduction in fossil fuels is larger than the increase in renewables, the overall
  impact of a higher oil price on investment in generation is negative
- *However, the introduction of the Kyoto protocol combined with higher fossil
  fuel prices enhances the probability of investing in renewables, thereby boosting overall PPP investment in generation.* This result shows the importance of
  legal international commitments to further generate confidence and foster
  investment
- *Private investors entering the market look more at market size than income
  level (the "affordability" level of consumers), but they look at both when determining how much to invest in generation.* This result raises concerns about the
  sustainability of such support mechanisms for renewables and their financing,
  particularly when the incremental costs implied by renewable-based generation
  are passed through to consumers.

Renewable-based Generation
Here, too, the results show strong evidence of the effectiveness of support
mechanisms.
The key results are:

- *The renewable energy market is strongly driven by supportive policies, which
  not only attract the entry of private investors but also determine the level of
  investment.* However, the influence of these policies over how much is invested
  could be much greater than it is suggesting the need to ensure that they are
  powerful enough and that they adequately allocate risks between the public
  and private sectors
- *However, economy-wide governance factors (control for corruption and
  degree of political competition) are considered by private investors mainly
  for taking the decision to enter into renewable-based generation, not what
  happens later.* This finding reinforces our belief that private investors seem to
  be adequately protected against risks, so that once they enter the market, they
  can accommodate the governance environment
- *Private investors also require technical and regulatory certainty about the
  availability of renewable-ready transmission resources.* The traditional
  reactive model of transmission regulation, where transmission is developed on
  a first-come, first-served basis is not conducive for renewables, as it introduces

extensive regulatory and technical uncertainty about whether adequate transmission will be available once the resource is generated—and transmission distances for renewables can be large
- *Private investors entering the market look more at market size than income level, whereas when determining the level of investment they assess both.* This finding parallels that found for overall generation and thus here, too, raises concerns about the sustainability of support mechanisms and their financing, particularly when the incremental costs implied by renewables are passed through to consumers.

In sum, private investors will assess the policy and regulatory regimes across all aspects of the project, not just the support or incentive mechanism. These aspects include the planning and approval process, given the potential for costly delays to construction that defer the point at which a project will start generating revenue; grid or infrastructure access and availability; and power purchase agreements.

Transmission and Distribution
The results show that regulatory governance is important in attracting and maintaining private investment in transmission and distribution (T&D).

The key results are:

- *Sectoral regulatory governance is crucial in attracting the entry of private investors in T&D, but it does not affect the level of investment.* This result suggests that, before entering the market, private investors value regulatory certainty. After entry, as the tariff formula is usually guaranteed in the medium term in their contracts, the presence of an autonomous regulator does not affect the level of investment. Another reason may be that implementation is less than optimal. Furthermore, as mentioned above for renewable-based generation, the traditional reactive model of transmission regulation, is not conducive to renewables
- *Similarly, economy-wide governance factors, including control for corruption and degree of political competition are factored in by private investors only in the initial stage of the game when the decision to enter into the T&D market is taken.* This finding again reinforces our suggestion that private investors seem to be adequately protected against their risks, so that once they have entered the market, they can accommodate the governance environment
- *The introduction of renewables in the power system enhanced overall PPP investment in T&D.* Renewable-based energy also requires technical and regulatory certainty about the availability of renewable-ready transmission resources
- *Private investors entering the T&D market look more at market size than income level, whereas when determining the level of investment in T&D they assess both the size and "affordability" level of consumers.* This finding parallels those for generation and renewable-based generation.

The bottom line is that sectoral governance—that is, support mechanisms, such as feed-in tariffs, and regulations—play a critical role in attracting private investment in generation, transmission, and distribution. Which incentive schemes work better than others in attracting PPP investment in renewables? The next chapter reviews case studies we did on China, Brazil, Mexico, and Peru to explore that question, along with the challenges of the transmission grid to integrate private investors into the system.

Notes

1. IEA analysis indicates that a 2–30 percent cut in the cost of renewable energy can result from improved design of incentive or support schemes, with the higher end of this range linked to projects with higher project risk, such as offshore wind.

2. The recent literature on regulatory governance for utility service industries has been pioneered by Levy and Spiller (1994).

3. http://www.ppiaf.org/ppiaf/page/private-participation-infrastructure-database

4. The six regions are East Asia and the Pacific (EAP), Europe and Central Asia (ECA), Latin America and the Caribbean (LAC), Middle East and North Africa (MNA), South Asia Region (SAR), and Sub-Saharan Africa (SSA).

5. The primary sector is energy, and the subsectors are electricity, natural gas, and other (road, telecom, or treatment plant). For the electricity subsector, the segment information tells whether it is a project for power generation, transmission, or distribution, or a combination of these. For a power generation project, the technology (fuel) indicates what fuel (coal, oil, or natural gas, etc.) or technology (hydro, wind, nuclear, etc.) is used for generation.

References

Burer, M. J., and R. Wustenhagen. 2009. "Which Renewable Energy Policy Is a Venture Capitalist's Best Friend? Empirical Evidence from a Survey of International Clean Tech Investors." *Energy Policy* 37: 4997–5006.

Cory, K., T. Couture, and C. Kreycik. 2009. *Feed-in Tariff Policy: Design, Implementation and RPS Policy Interactions*. Technical Report NREL/TP-6A2-45549. http://www.nrel.gov/docs/fy09osti/45549.pdf.

Couture, T. D., K. Cory, C. Kreycik, and E. Williams. 2010. *A Policymaker's Guide to Feed-in Tariff Policy Design*. NREL. http://www.energy.eu/publications/A_Policymakers_Guide_to_Feedin_Tariffs_NREL.pdf.

Cubbin, J., and J. Stern. 2006. "The Impact of Regulatory Governance and Privatization on Electricity Industry Capacity in Developing Countries." *World Bank Economic Review* 20 (1): 115–41.

DB Climate Change Advisors. 2010. *Global Energy Transfer Feed-in tariff for Developing countries*. New York: DB Climate Change Advisors.

Econ Poyry. 2008. "The Electricity Sector in Georgia a Risk Assessment." Commissioned by the Ministry of Energy Georgia.

Elders, I., Ault, G., Galloway, S., McDonald, J., Kohler, J., Leach, M. and L. Enteric. 2006. "Electricity Network Scenarios for the United Kingdom in 2050," in T. Jamasb,

W. J. Nuttall and M. G. Pollitt (eds.) *Future Electricity Technologies and Systems*, Cambridge: Cambridge University Press, pp. 24–79.

Greacen, C., N. Kahyoza, and A. Mbawala. 2010. "Towards Light Handed Regulation for Small Power Producers in Tanzania." draft, World Bank and PPIAF. Washington, DC: World Bank.

IEA (International Energy Agency). 2010. *World Energy Outlook 2010*. Paris: IEA.

Joskow, P. 2008. "Incentive Regulation and its Application to Electricity Networks." *Review of Network Economics* 7 (4): 547–60.

Lesser, J., and X. Su. 2008. "Design of an Economically Efficient Feed-in Tariff Structure for Renewable Energy Development." *Energy Policy* 36: 981–90.

Levy, B., and P. T. Spiller. 1994. "The Institutional Foundations of Regulatory Commitment: A Comparative Analysis of Telecommunications Regulation." *The Journal of Law, Economics & Organisation* 10: 201–46.

Lipp, J. 2007. "Lessons for Effective Renewable Electricity Policy from Denmark, Germany and the United Kingdom." *Energy Policy* 35: 5481–95.

Luis, A., J. L. Guasch, and S. L. Azumendi. 2008. "Regulatory Governance and Sector Performance Methodology and Evaluation for Electricity Distribution in Latin America," World Bank Policy Research Working Paper 4494.

Menanteau, P., F. Dominique, and M. Lamy. 2003. "Price versus Quantities: Choosing Policies for Promoting the Development of Renewable Energy." *Energy Policy* 31: 799–812.

Mitchell, C., D. Bauknecht, and P. M. Connor. 2006. "Effectiveness through Risk Reduction: A Comparison of the Renewable Obligation in England and Wales and the Feed-In System in Germany." *Energy Policy* 34: 297–305.

OFGEM (Office of the Gas and Electricity Markets). 2010. *Project Discovery Options for Delivering Secure and Sustainable Energy Supplies*. Ref.16/10. London: OFGEM.

REN21. 2011. *Renewables 2011, Global Status Report*. http://www.ren21.net/globalstatusreport/REN21_GSR_2011_full.pdf.

Rickerson, W., and R. C. Grace. 2007. "The Debate over Fixed Price Incentives for Renewable Electricity in Europe and the United States: Fallout and Future Directions." The Heinrich Boll Foundation. http://www.futurepolicy.org/fileadmin/user_upload/PACT/Learn_more/Rickerson_Grace_2007_.pdf

United Nations Environment Programme (UNEP), Sustainable Energy Finance Initiative (SEFI) and Bloomberg New Energy Finance. 2011. *Global Trends in Sustainable Energy Investment 2010*. Geneva, Switzerland: UNEP.

Vagliasindi, M. 2012a. "Key Drivers of PPPs in Electricity Generation in Developing Countries: Cross-Country Evidence of Switching between PPP Investment in Fossil Fuel and Renewable-Based Generation." World Bank Policy Research Working Paper 6118. Washington, DC.

———. 2012b. "The Role of Policy Driven Incentives to Attract PPPs in Renewable-Based Energy in Developing Countries: A Cross-Country Analysis." World Bank Policy Research Working Paper 6120, World Bank, Washington, DC.

———. 2012c. "The Role of Regulatory Governance in Driving PPPs in Electricity Transmission and Distribution in Developing Countries: A Cross-Country Analysis." Policy Research Working Paper 6121, World Bank, Washington, DC.

CHAPTER 3

Renewable Energy Case Studies

Renewable energy support and incentive mechanisms are the most important factors driving the growth of a market in renewable-based energy—and they can come in many forms:

- **Price-based support**. The most popular is a feed-in tariff (FIT), favored by a majority of European countries (such as Germany and Spain) and widely used in developing countries. This system sets a guaranteed price for renewable energy generation or an addition to the prevailing market price
- **Quota-based support**. The most common is a Renewable Portfolio Standard (RPS), favored by the United States, Canada, and India. It typically requires power utilities to use a given proportion of electricity from renewables, and it is often combined with mandates for utilities to meet obligations through trading Renewable Energy Certificates (also called Tradable Green Certificates)
- **Fiscal incentives**. These typically include tax breaks and capital subsidies
- **Financial supports**. These typically involve public investment, loans, or financing.

What is the emerging experience with these mechanisms to date? Typically, feed-in tariffs—despite offering simplicity—tend to be set on the high side, because they induce generators to choose high-cost sites and provide fewer incentives than other mechanisms for cost cuts. This problem illustrates the importance of designing an efficient energy support system, which not only promotes diffusion but also provides continuous incentives for cost-reducing innovations. In contrast, competitive auctions have tended to be low initially and are not always the most-effective instrument for renewables, but they allow for a discovery effect to determine the market-based feed-in tariff to attract private investment.

How do these mechanisms influence public-private partnerships (PPPs) in the power sector in the developing world? And what role should PPPs play in efficiently expanding a transmission network system with natural monopoly characteristics and thus subject to public regulation? To answer these questions we undertook a study of four country cases that present a wide range of schemes aimed at promoting renewable energies, different ownership (fully private or public or a mix) and market structures, and different levels of renewable energy

Table 3.1 Case Study Taxonomy

	Ownership	Market structure	Incentives/mechanisms to promote renewable energies	Renewable energy penetration
China	Mainly state-owned.	Organizational unbundling	Mainly feed-in tariffs	17% of total electricity installed capacity (15.7% of hydro, 0.7% of wind, and 0.6% of biomass) 2011 data
Mexico	Mainly state-owned.	Vertically inte-grated structure	Open Season mechanism to connect renewable energy to the trans-mission network. The state utility builds the infrastructure based on RE developers' interest. RE producers pay for the infrastructure	16.6% of total electricity production (16.5% of hydro, 0.1% of wind) 2008 data.
Brazil	Mixed public and private owned (30% in the distribu-tion sector, 90% in the gen-eration sector, and almost 100% in the transmission segment).	Single buyer model through a central-ized purchasing entity	Move from feed-in tariffs (ProInfra) to auctions.	82% of total electricity production (77% of hydro, 5% of biomass) 2010 data.
Peru	70% of total electricity capacity is generated by private companies. In the transmission segment, all companies are private. In the distribution sector the State and the private sector have similar levels of participation.	Ownership unbundling	Use of auctions as a way of incentivizing the use of renewable energy. So far, 2 auctions have taken place.	60% of total electricity production (almost all renewable energy in Peru comes from hydro sources; only a small percentage, 0.7 MW, comes from wind). 2009 data.

penetration (table 3.1). For example, in terms of incentives, China has moved from auctioning to feed-in tariffs, Mexico has done the reverse, and Brazil and Peru are using competitive auctions.

The Case of China

Electricity Market Reforms

In 2002, the Chinese government dismantled the monopoly State Power Corporation (SPC) into separate generation, transmission, and service units (U.S. Energy Information Administration). Since then, China's electricity generation sector has been dominated by five state-owned holding companies: China Huaneng Group, China Datang Group, China Huandian, Guodian Power, and China Power Investment. The remaining generators are independent producers, which often partner with privately listed arms of state-owned companies.

While the generation sector has some market competition, the transmission and distribution sectors are heavily state-owned and controlled. During the 2002 reforms, SPC divested all of its electricity transmission and distribution assets into two new companies, the Southern company and the State Power Grid Company. The government also established a national power regulator, the State Electricity Commission (SERC).

Generation

In 2009 China had an estimated total installed electricity generating capacity of 874 gigawatts—74.6 percent of which came from conventional thermal sources, mostly coal (figure 3.1). That capacity is expected to grow a lot in the next decade to meet rising demand, particularly from demand centers in the eastern and southern parts of the country.

China's goal is to generate at least 15 percent of total energy output with renewable energy sources by 2020, as the government shifts to a less-resource intense economy—a goal it has already met with renewables now accounting for 17 percent (table 3.2). In 2009, China became the second largest producer of

Figure 3.1 Fossil Fuels Dominate Production and Capacity

a. Coal, Oil & Gas, Nuclear, Hydro, and Wind electricity production 3663 TWh, 2009

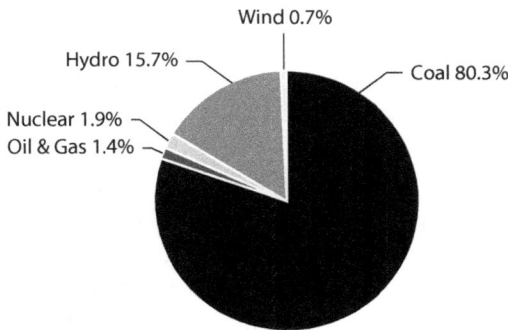

b. Fossil Fuels, Nuclear, Hydro, and Wind installed capacity 874 GW, 2009

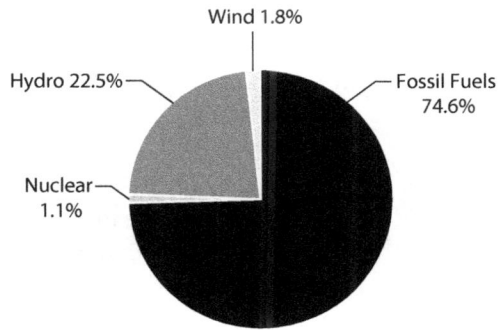

Wind 0.7%
Hydro 15.7%
Coal 80.3%
Nuclear 1.9%
Oil & Gas 1.4%

Wind 1.8%
Hydro 22.5%
Fossil Fuels 74.6%
Nuclear 1.1%

Source: Cheung 2011.

Table 3.2 Renewables Take up 17 Percent of China's Energy Mix

participation of renewables in China's energy mix, 2009

	Total installed capacity (GW)	Total electricity production (TWh)	Share of total electricity production (%)
Hydro	196.8	574.7	15.7
Wind	16.1	26.9	0.7
Solar	0.3	0.5	—
Biomass	4.0	20	0.6
Total	217.3	620.6	17.00

Source: Cheung 2011.
Note: — = not applicable.

hydroelectric power, generating 575 terawatt-hours of electricity from hydroelectric sources—15.7 percent of total generation. Installed hydroelectric generating capacity was around 197 gigawatts in 2009, accounting for over 20 percent
of total installed capacity. Wind is the second leading renewable source of power
generation, with 0.7 percent, and biomass is third with 0.6 percent (table 3.2).
However, despite significant efforts to diversify its energy mix, China's dependence on coal and fixed electricity tariffs have provoked major outages.
Although coal prices have more than doubled in the past decade, electricity
tariffs have only increased by a third. Making matters worse has been an unusu-
ally severe drought.

Transmission

Investment shortages in electricity transmission and distribution have become
the bottleneck of power development in China. During the 8th, 9th, and 10th
Five-Year-Plans the shares of investments in transmission and distribution were
13.7 percent, 37.3 percent, and 30 percent—significantly below the 50 percent
average of developed countries. Nevertheless, investment levels have been growing consistently. In 2006, total investment in power grids construction was 210.6
billion renmibi (RMB), up 38 percent from 2005; in 2007, it reached 245.1
billon RMB, up another 16.4 percent. That same year, the national average line
loss rate was 6.97 percent, down 0.07 percent from 2006 (In-depth Investment
Report on Power Grid Industry of China, 2009).

Renewable Energy Reforms

Renewable energy planning in China took place through two phases
(REN21 2011):

- *Phase One (1996–2000):* Use research and development and demonstration
  projects to elevate most renewable energy technologies to a level near or equal
  to advanced international standards. Commercialize some of the mature technologies, extend their application, and develop markets gradually. Improve on
  traditional, low-efficiency biomass energy consumption by making wider use
  of wind, solar, and hydro energy to help electrify remote areas and islands
- *Phase Two (2000–10):* Disseminate renewable energy technology on a wider
  scale; create advanced, international standard industrial and technology research
  systems; achieve large-scale production; and increase the total development and
  use of all new and renewable energy sources from 300 million tonne of coal
  equivalent (tce) at present to 390 million tce.

Of all the measures taken, it was the implementation of the 2005 Renewable
Energy Law on January 1, 2006 that gave an unprecedented impulse to renewable energies. The renewable energy sector boomed, resulting in China taking a
leading position globally, particularly in wind power, solar water heating, and
small hydropower. The law provides four schemes (1) a cost-sharing scheme

that requires that additional costs of renewable energy generation are shared by electricity end-users through a surcharge, (2) a feed-in tariff scheme, (3) a mandatory grid-connection system that requires grid operators to buy all electricity generated from renewable sources, and (4) a national target system that sets strategic objectives to achieve 10 percent of renewables in primary energy use by 2010 and 15 percent by 2020 (Renewable Energy Policy Network for the 21st Century 2009).

Another landmark for renewables was the Medium and Long Term Development Plan for Renewable Energy 2007. It outlined a Renewable Portfolio Standard (RPS) target, stating that in areas covered by large-scale power grids, the non-hydro renewables share of total generation will reach 1 percent by 2010 and exceed 3 percent by 2020. The government also established the Renewable Energy Fund to cover the gap between the cost of the feed-in tariffs paid to generators and the prices paid by consumers as well as the additional capital costs of transmission extensions. The 2009 Renewable Energy Law amendments expanded the uses to include subsidizing the grid companies for the costs of integrating renewable energy that they cannot recover from electricity sales to consumers.

The big push for wind power came when the National Development and Reform Commission (NDRC) initiated the wind power concession program to introduce competition, relying on bid based off-take prices. In 2003, it launched the first concession tender, mandating turbine local content to promote the country's wind industry. From 2003 to 2008, five concession tenders were organized, first mandating 50 percent local content, then 70 percent. However this requirement was later removed because it was construed as a breach of World Trade Organization rules. The electricity off-take price was theoretically determined by the winning bid price up to 30,000 hours of full load operation and at the average network electricity price for generation exceeding that amount. The contract is for 25 years. The lowest bid (later changed to the closest price to the average of the bidding price with the highest proportion of local content) is awarded the concession projects.

Since 2005, and despite the global financial crisis, China's installed wind capacity has increased to about 45 gigawatts in 2010 from 1.3 gigawatts in 2005 (figure 3.2). In fact, in 2009, the wind power industry was among the few new industries to stimulate the world economy toward recovery—with global investment exceeding US$60 billion, of which China alone accounted for over US$20 billion (China Wind Power Outlook 2010). Globally, newly installed capacity of global wind power rose by 42 percent, and in China, by 166 percent over the 2008/09 period.

Analysts predict that China's base of wind power installations will total 50–60 gigawatts by 2015 and 80–100 gigawatts by 2020. The 2020 goal was revised upward fourfold from the 30 gigawatts goal set by the Mid to Long-Term Development Plan for Renewable Energy, promulgated by Beijing in September 2007. Moreover, experts and government officials predict that

Figure 3.2 China's Installed Wind Power Capacity Has Skyrocketed

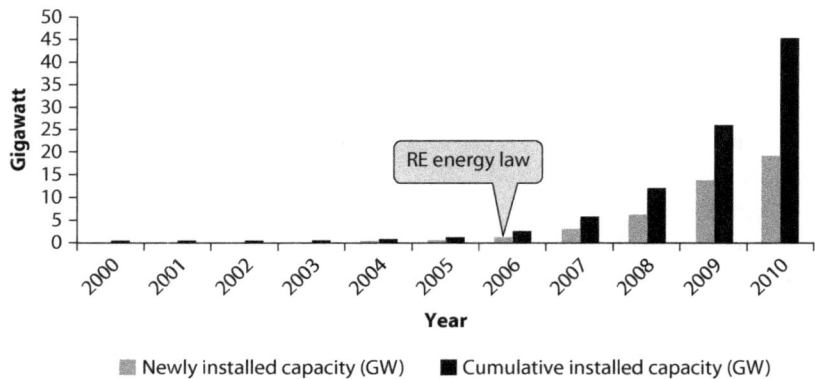

Source: Junfeng et al. 2010; REN21 2011.

domestic installed wind-power capacity may reach as high as 100–150 gigawatts by 2020 (Renewable Energy Policy Network 2009).

Incentives to Promote Renewable Energy

Under the 2005 Renewable Energy Law, China has implemented a number of pricing mechanisms and cost arrangements. There are different pricing schemes for different technologies—and pricing arrangements for wind and solar have changed over time as these technologies developed.

Cost-plus. This approach—currently used for geothermal, and tidal power—involves setting a price for a particular project on the principle of reasonable production cost plus reasonable profit. It presents significant uncertainty for project developers, but is favored by the central government to stimulate nascent technologies (Tawney *et al.* 2011).

Concessions. This is basically a competitive tender model, asking project developers to compete for long-term power purchase agreements, with price and domestic content as the key criteria. The NDRC held five bidding rounds between 2003 and 2007 for 3.35 gigawatts of onshore wind capacity and some provinces followed suit. The concession approach is still used for offshore wind, but it has led to downward price pressure and unprofitable onshore wind generation, deterring further private capital investment. The state-owned generation companies were able to support their losses in wind through indirect state budget support and thus dominate the existing wind installed base (Tawney *et al.* 2011).

Feed-in tariff. With this approach, the NDRC sets the rates that all generators can charge the grid companies for the electricity they provide to the grid. The interesting feature of the Chinese system is that originally the prices established from the competitive bidding were used to set feed-in tariff rates. In other countries the levels of feed-in tariffs are usually set based on market analysis, surveys, industry research, and consultations with the public. In China, where the renewable energy sector undergoes rapid changes—costs decrease quickly owing to technology improvements, increased efficiencies, and economies of scale—it would have been quite difficult to administratively set a fixed price without information from the bidding process.

For wind power, in 2009 the government set nationwide guidance on the tariff—replacing the project-by-project cost-plus and the concession models, with guarantees for 20 years. Regions with poorer wind resources are paid a higher tariff to ensure profitability despite their lower productivity. Ranging from 0.51 Yuan per kilowatt-hour to 0.61 Yuan per kilowatt-hour (US$0.075 per kilowatt-hour to US$0.090 per kilowatt-hour), the rates are significantly higher than the average 0.34 Yuan per kilowatt-hour (US$0.05 per kilowatt-hour) paid to coal-fired generators. The rates are also significantly higher than the concession tariffs had been. (Tawney et al. 2011).

For solar PV power, prior to 2009, when the market was small, the approved feed-in tariff rate was applied on an individual project basis and ranged between RMB4-9 (US$0.58–1.32) per kilowatt-hour. Since early 2009, the government has established price regulation with a concession program in Western China's Dunhuang region. In August 2011 the NDRC announced the first national level feed-in tariff program for solar power. A feed-in tariff for the projects approved before July 1, 2011 or completed by December 31, 2011 is RMB 1.15 (US cent 17.9) per kilowatt-hour, excluding solar thermal. The tariff for the projects approved after July 1, 2011 and not completed by December 31, 2011 is RMB 1.00 per kilowatt-hour (US cent 15.5) (Bloomberg News 2011).

For biomass power, a feed-in tariff is provided for all projects. In 2008, the subsidy of RMB 0.25 (US cent 3.7) per kilowatt-hour for a 15 year period was increased to RMB0.35 (US cent 5.1) per kilowatt-hour.

Challenges

Feed-in tariffs design. China's feed-in tariff system has been criticized for being too complex and difficult to understand, especially for international investors. Some have suggested establishing a fixed-price structure for each technology based on its specific characteristics such as resource potential and geographical distribution (Renewable Energy Policy Network 2009).

Development of the transmission grid. The rapid development of renewable energies in China (especially wind power) has put unprecedented strain on the country's electricity grid infrastructure. In the past four years, China has doubled its wind turbine installations—accounting for more than half of the world wind energy market. However, the country has built turbines so quickly that it failed to keep up with construction and most turbines have not been connected to the energy grid.

To smooth out the load variability, grid companies realize that it is imperative to take two interrelated measures (1) overcome the geographic mismatch of demand and supply by building additional power transmission lines to handle the transmission of larger quantities of electricity and (2) strengthen the interconnections between regional grids (Cheung 2011). In March 2010, Premier Wen Jiabao announced a plan to build a "unified strong and smart grid" system nationwide by 2020, which should incorporate energy supplies from various sources.

Transmission costs. Renewable energy generators are not required to pay for the transmission infrastructure necessary to carry their power to load centers. Grid companies pay for the transmission expansion directly and are required to connect any renewable energy generation within their geographic region that meets minimum requirements. Grid companies are partially reimbursed through a government subsidy based on the distance between the generation site and the main grid infrastructure (Tawney *et al.* 2011). However, the rates they can charge consumers are set as a part of China's larger economic policy, and there is no guaranteed rate of return to the grid companies (Tawney *et al.* 2011).

In China, the cost sharing model has not ensured that expansion keeps pace with the growth of renewables. The cost structure is very advantageous to renewable energy developers, but under the feed-in tariff model they indirectly pay the price for the lack of transmission investment when they cannot sell their electricity into the grid (Tawney *et al.* 2011).

The Case of Brazil

Electricity Market Reforms

The first phase of reforms took place between 1996 and 2001, when the largest state-owned enterprise (ELETROBRAS) was unbundled into six holding corporations and 14 generation and transmission companies. By 2001 more than 80 percent of the electricity sold in the country was conducted by privatized distributing companies (Jannuzzi 2004). However, generation remained dominated by state owned companies, with a 70 percent share, and transmission was left in state hands. In addition, the government established a number of new institutions, such as the National Electricity Regulatory Agency (ANEEL).

The second phase of reforms began in 2003, right after Brazil's worst energy crisis, which largely stemmed from several years of drier than average weather. The government of Inacio Lula Da Silva introduced a second "wave" of power market reforms ("new model") to improve incentives for installing new generation capacity, create more competitive conditions, and improve the institutional framework. The main characteristics of this new model were:

- Less emphasis on the short-term "spot" market as a provider of signals for system expansion and more emphasis on the forward contract market to induce additions of new generation capacity
- A requirement for mandatory energy auctions for distributions companies to cover 100 percent of all loads. Distributors could acquire energy only through contract auctions for long-term contracts (3–5 years) to reduce

risks for generation investors and promote competition. Benchmark prices were used for pass-through of wholesale power costs to consumers procured under the new energy auctions, as supply costs reflect the average price of all contracts.

The two models differed greatly. The original reform model (implemented in 1995) focused on opening up the power market with an emphasis on privatizing all companies. System expansion was supposed to be achieved through short-term price signals and contracting obligations. The new model (implemented in 2004), however, emphasizes coexistence between state-owned and private companies.

Impact of Auctions on Electricity Transmission

The introduction of auctions—the first was held in December 2004, with contracts for a total of about 40 gigawatts traded—significantly affected the transmission sector, whose expansion has since been driven largely by private investors. Public firms also participate in auctions, sometimes as individual firms, but more often joining a private consortium with less than 50 percent of its capital. The main advantages of these PPPs are (1) each firm takes advantage of its expertise; (2) line construction is faster and cheaper because the concessionaires are not constrained by the federal auctions law; and (3) assets are located within concession areas of these public firms, so they can more easily maintain the lines and substations after construction.

Private investors have dominated transmission auctions both in terms of number of projects and levels of investment (Serrato 2008) (figure 3.3). From 1999 to 2007, private investors acquired 38 enterprises, while public firms acquired 17, and PPPs, 12. Their dominance is even more evident if we look at average revenue (RAP) bids—about R$26 million for private investors and only R$7.4 million for public firms. In fact, private investors received more than 75 percent of total auction revenues. Moreover, if PPPs are considered private, this percentage increases at least 7 percent, reaching more than 83 percent of the total RAP to private companies.[1]

Figure 3.3.a Private Investors Dominate Auctions in Number of Firms Acquired (1999–2007)

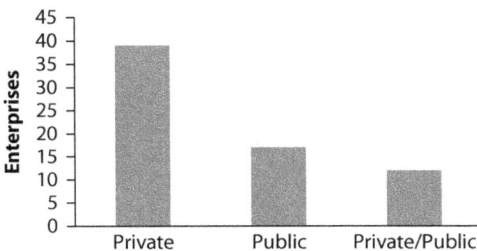

Figure 3.3. b and Average Revenue Offered (1997–2007)

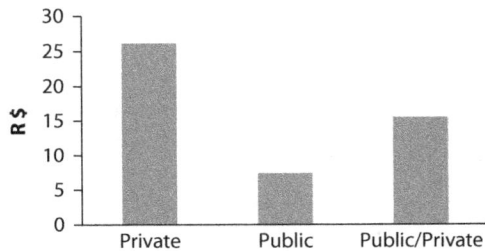

Source: Serrato 2008.

Incentives to Promote Renewable Energy

Brazil's energy mix is largely renewable, with around 84 percent of electricity generated from renewable energy sources. Most electricity (77 percent) is produced by large hydro power plants that utilize extensive freshwater reservoirs (figure 3.4). And hydro has far more installed capacity than any other energy sources (figure 3.5). But in recent years, nonconventional sources such as wind

Figure 3.4 Renewables Lead the Energy Mix

electricity generation by source

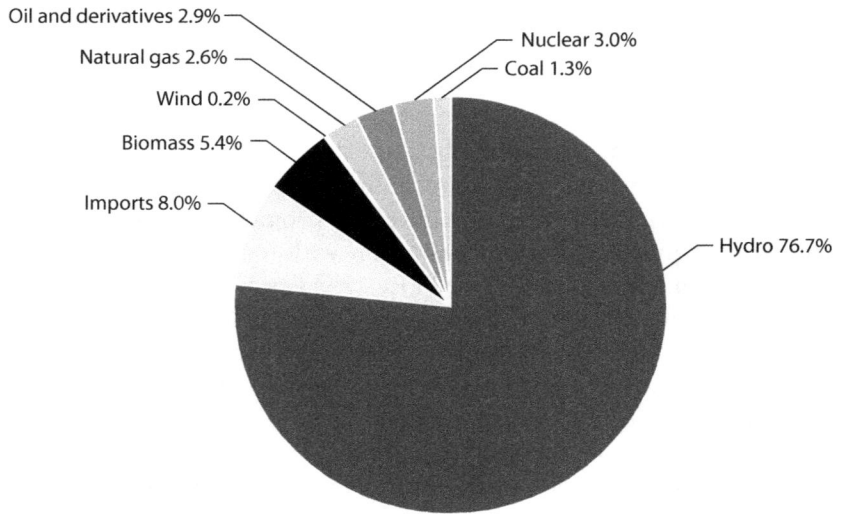

Oil and derivatives 2.9%
Natural gas 2.6%
Wind 0.2%
Biomass 5.4%
Imports 8.0%
Nuclear 3.0%
Coal 1.3%
Hydro 76.7%

Source: EPE.

Figure 3.5 Hydro Has by Far the Most Installed Electricity Capacity

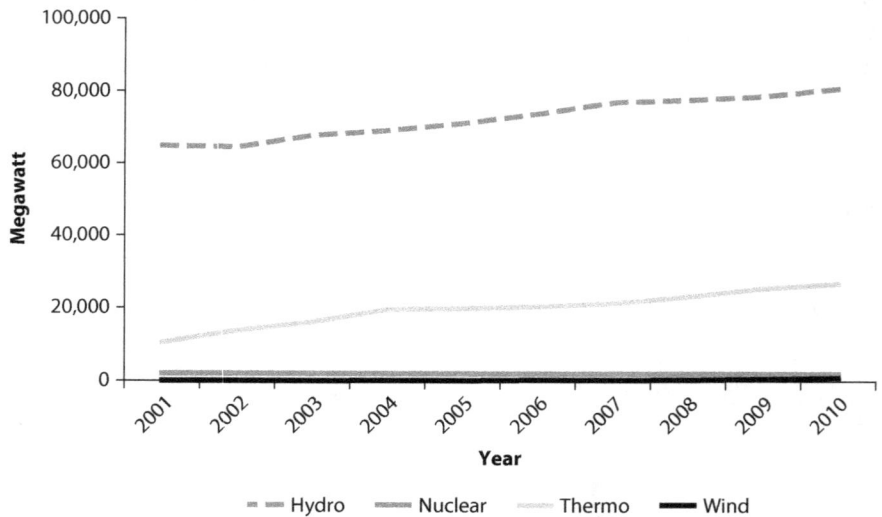

Hydro   Nuclear   Thermo   Wind

Source: ANEEL 2011.

and biomass have emerged—a response to new incentives, including feed-in tariffs, discounts, and auctions.

Feed-in tariffs. The PROINFA. program, launched in 2002 was the country's first scheme to foster renewable energy sources, although it was not considered effectives and has been discontinued. It was essentially a feed-in tariff designed to contract 3,300 megawatts of wind, biomass, and small hydro by 2006. Each renewable source had a quota of 1,100 megawatts but a different tariff. Electrobras (a state-owned holding company of power utilities) purchased the energy produced by participating plants through 20-year contracts, then resold the energy to all consumers in proportion to actual consumption. Consumers were entitled to portions of PROINFA energy in their contract portfolios. However, the program was criticized for lacking economic signals for efficiency and technological improvement and for poorly performing projects.

Discounts. In 2007, Brazil established discounts on transmission and distribution for non-regulated (free) consumers (generally large industrial groups) who purchased energy through contracts backed up by renewable sources. In practice, the system is a cross-subsidy on the "wires" cost, paid by all captive consumers and received by the free consumers who purchase renewable energy. The incentive has been so effective that it has induced the installation of at least 700 megawatts of small scale renewable source based capacity in the period 2006–09 (mainly small scale hydropower, but also bioelectricity). The main criticism is that it introduces a market distortion because regulated consumers directly subsidize the incremental cost.

Auctions. This mechanism was introduced to reconcile risk reduction for new investors with efficient energy procurement for regulated users. There are several types of auctions. One is for developing specific technologies or projects. Another type, known as "reserve energy auctions," is aimed at increasing the reserve margin and ensuring security of supply. The reserve auctions are fully specified by the government, including the definition of the technology (or project) and the demand volume to be contracted.

The first technology-specific "reserve energy" auction was in August 2008 to contract new energy from sugarcane bagasse cogeneration ("bioelectricity") for delivery in 2011 and 2012. It was motivated by the country's ethanol "boom" in 2006/07, which fostered the expansion of the sugarcane production and the installation of hundreds of new ethanol mills that were set to start operations between 2009 and 2012. Approximately 60 percent of the gross capacity was sold in the auction (1,500 megawatts or 4,800 gigawatt-hour per year) for an average price of US$80 per megawatt-hour. The net energy cost to the consumer—which depends on the expected revenue resulting from participation in the spot market—is expected to reach US$50 per megawatt-hour assuming a yearly energy spot price of about US$30 per megawatt-hour over the contract term. Some 2,700 gigawatt-hour per year of bioelectricity is still available to be sold in future auctions or directly to free consumers.

A similar auction to contract wind power for delivery in 2012 was carried out in December 2009, when the government tried to take advantage of lower equipment costs (resulting from the global financial crisis) to develop wind-based generation on a larger scale (figure 3.6). The 20-year energy contract had an accounting mechanism designed to provide investors with a fixed payment (for financing purposes) while managing the quantity-price risk and incentivizing/penalizing production above/below a given firm energy threshold. In this contract, investors offer a reference price value (megawatt-hour per year) and consumers pay a fixed value for the production *ex-ante*. The "reference value" is monitored, and penalties or incentives for over and under production are applied. The final average price was US$82 per megawatt-hour, 22 percent below the initial price, and lower than what most analysts had estimated. About 1,800 megawatts of capacity was traded, with a diverse mix of investors (local and foreign private generators, manufacturers, and government-owned companies) winning the contracts. Three new wind turbine factories are to be installed.

In August 2010, a new reserve energy auction for renewables was carried out. An installed capacity of 2,900 megawatts was contracted, including 70 wind farms, 12 sugarcane cogeneration plants, and 7 small hydros. The contracting of wind-based capacity reached 2,050 megawatts at an average rate of US$75 per megawatt-hour. Biomass came to 713 megawatts at an average rate of US$82 per megawatt-hour and small hydro power reached 132 megawatts at an average rate of US$81 per megawatt-hour.

How do the PROINFA and renewable energy specific auctions compare? Although the annual costs of both mechanisms is practically the same (around US$1 billion), the energy auction scheme is expected to deliver 20 percent more total capacity with an average 25 percent lower energy cost and an expected 60 percent lower tariff. In the case of bioelectricity, plants acquired through the auction scheme exhibited higher efficiencies.

However, the very low prices (in the lower bound, but not outside the range of international feed-in tariffs) that have resulted in the renewables auctions

Figure 3.6 Wind Generation in Brazil is on the Rise

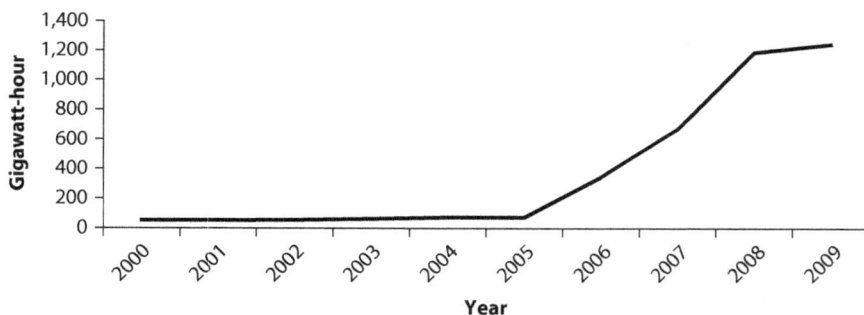

Source: EPE 2011.

raise concerns about whether bid winners will be able to construct plants and profit from them. Although the auction system includes a number of pre-requisites to avoid speculative behavior among participants and lower the risk of construction delays or no construction of facilities at all, the use of a relevant set of financial, technical, and operational guarantees is still lacking.

Nevertheless, as of August 2010, Brazil has successfully conducted 31 auctions for existing and new energy, with about 26,000 megawatts of new capacity contracted for delivery dates between 2008 and 2015, and contract terms ranging from 15 to 30 years. This includes about 8,700 megawatts of new renewable capacity and 17,500 megawatts of large hydro plants in the Amazon region. Of the total new generation capacity, 49 percent has been allocated to hydro resources, 44 percent to thermal resources, and the remaining 8 percent to biomass and wind power.

The Case of Peru

Electricity Market Reforms
From 1991 to 1993, Peru undertook a major restructuring of its power sector that reflected regional and global trends—unbundling the national electricity utility into three main segments: generation, transmission, and distribution. The rationale was to include the private sector to gain higher levels of efficiency and service quality, but leave the public sector responsible for policy formulation and regulation.

Private companies emerging from the 1992 reforms made substantial investment commitments that were fulfilled in the following years. Investment figures reached their highest levels in the period 1996–99, then declined after the transition period (figure 3.7). High levels of investment led to annual average increases in installed capacity of 9.2 percent, a rate that was not matched by higher demand (annual average increases of only 4.7 percent). Investments in transmission and distribution led to increases in coverage from 53 percent in 1993 to 76 percent in 2004.

However, the privatization push came to an end in May 2002, when under strong regional opposition and public outcry, the government cancelled the privatization of Egasa and Egesur, the two public-owned generating companies serving Arequipa, Moquegua and Tacna. At this point, generation (90 percent of companies) and transmission (100 percent) are managed to a great extent by private enterprises (figure 3.8). But in distribution, public (48 percent of investments) and private (52 percent) investment are almost even.

Institutional responsibilities rest on the Ministry of Energy and Mining and the Regulator of Private Investment in Energy (OSINERG). The former is responsible for approving concessions, sector planning, and rule-making. The latter is accountable for implementing the tariff structure. Law 26.734, which is the statutory instrument of OSINERG, establishes the regulator's responsibility, which is to oversee service quality, efficiency, and investment commitments.

Figure 3.7 Privatization Led to an Investment Surge in the Second Half of the 1990s

total investment in electricity in Peru (US$ million)

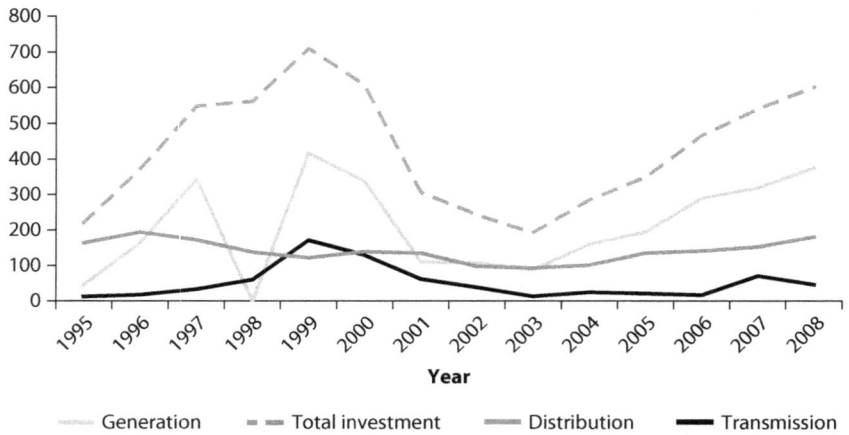

Source: Ministry of Mining and Energy of Peru Sector Eléctrico en Peru, various years.

Figure 3.8 Private Investors Dominate Generation and Transmission

by type of ownership in Peru, US$ million

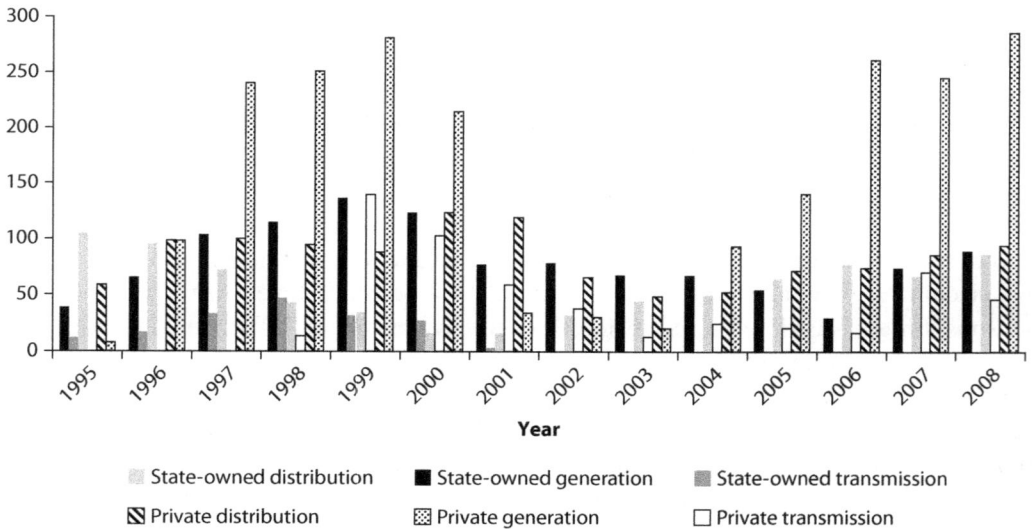

Source: Ministry of Mining and Energy of Peru Sector Eléctrico en Peru, various years.

Generation

By 2009, total system generation was 30,915 gigawatt-hour. The main energy source is hydropower, representing close to 63 percent of all the electricity generated (figure 3.9)—a high percentage but far lower than the record hit in 2001, when it represented 89 percent. The turnaround for hydro began in 2002 with the discovery of major natural gas reserves in Camisea. Since then, the share of

Figure 3.9 Hydro and Natural Gas Dominate Generation
by type of fuel (GWh)

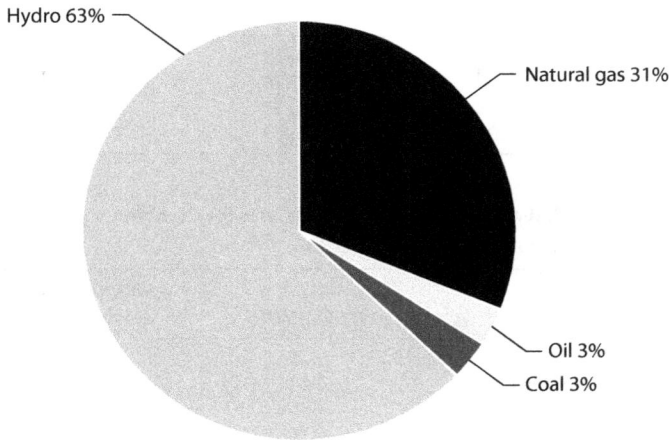

natural gas-fired thermal generation in the country's energy mix has shot up from about 10 percent in 2001 to 31.1 percent in 2009. Coal accounts for a 3.1 percent share, and oil, 2.9 percent.

Over the past decade, electricity power demand has jumped from 2.621 megawatts in 2000 to a peak of 4,322 megawatts in 2009, although the recent financial crisis has slowed the rise somewhat in 2008/09. Electricity consumption has also risen sharply—in fact, more quickly than for demand—from 15.546 gigawatt-hour in 2000 to 27,249 gigawatt-hour in 2009, but a slowdown in this growth is similarly evident in 2008/09 because of the financial crisis. Between 2012 and 2020, it is estimated that Peru will need to increase to 6,140 megawatts to handle demand that is growing by 9 percent per year.

The Peruvian electricity sector is strongly linked and dependent on natural gas from the Camisea gas field, with relatively large reserves. Although legally the hydrocarbon sector is part of a competitive market, the government has a strong interest in setting policies for internal consumption and prices, and conditions for exporting.

The Camisea natural gas price for internal use in power generation is one of the cheapest in the region, essentially a discounted internal price for all types of consumption, especially power generation. This low level creates a distortion in the power market that discourages developing alternative generation like hydro-electricity—as well as the efficient use of natural gas in thermal power generation, such as through combine cycle units. As table 3.3a.a shows, the 2008 Camisea natural gas price for power generation for each of the four main thermal power plants (either in or close to metropolitan Lima area) is around US$2.2 per million British Thermal Unit (BTU). This price, as table 3.3b shows, is below that of other countries and the resulting electricity energy cost for combine-cycle units. Camisea's installed capacity has skyrocketed thanks to low prices (see figure 3.10).

Table 3.3a Lima-Based Gas Prices Average only US$2.2 per Million BTU ...

natural gas prices for power generation, 2008 (US$/MMBTU)

Item	Ventanilla	Santa rosa	Chilca	Kallpa
Field	1.3065	1.3753	1.3753	1.3961
Transport	0.7398	0.7398	0.7392	0.7402
Distribution	0.1218	0.1218	0.0	0.0
Total	2.1681	2.2369	2.1145	2.1363

Table 3.3b. Far Below that of Other Countries and Costs for Combine-Cycle Units

natural gas prices (site of generation) (US$/MMBTU)

Country	Gas price, (US$/MMBTU)	Corresponding CCGT generation variable cost, (US cents/kWh)
Vietnam	3.20	2.24
Georgia (imports from GAZPROM)	3.50	2.45
Azerbaijan (imports from Russia)	6.77	4.74
USA, October 2007 Henry hub spot price	7.02	4.91

Source: Mercados.

In addition, recent preliminary World Bank's studies[2] indicate that the economic netback price (at the field) for Camisea natural gas that is used for alternative processes (other than power generation)—like petrochemical, liquefied natural gas, or industrial use) are in the range of US$5 per One Million BTU (MMBTU) for liquefied natural gas[3] (for supply to Mexico) to about US$9 per MMBTU for industry replacing liquid fuels. The thermal generation production cost is about 3.5 cents of US$ per kilowatt-hour, making most potential hydropower projects uncompetitive.

The official Ministry of Energy and Mining (MEM) energy policy is that the promotional internal price of Camisea natural gas should be maintained at least for the period (5 years) stipulated in the renegotiated contract with the producers (which allows for no more than a 5 percent increase in the price of natural gas annually, and not larger than the percentage increase of liquid fuels), and after that, the annual increases should be lower than the percentage increase of liquid fuels. In any case, the initial price gap will persist in the future. This price policy applies to the initial fields of Camisea (known as lots 88 and 56), but not to any other exploitations of natural gas fields in the same area of Camisea or in other places.

Transmission

The transmission of electricity in Peru is provided by seven private enterprises. In 1998, the grid was integrated with the construction (through a Build-Operate-Transfer (BOT) concession) of the Mantaro-Socabaya transmission line,[4] which unified the two largest grid systems. After the unification, the government established the National Interconnected System, which included 20 out of the 24 states of Peru, with annual energy production of 18.800 gigawatts and a total demand of 2.800 megawatts. The main transmission network

Figure 3.10 Camisea's Installed Capacity Has Skyrocketed Thanks to Low Prices

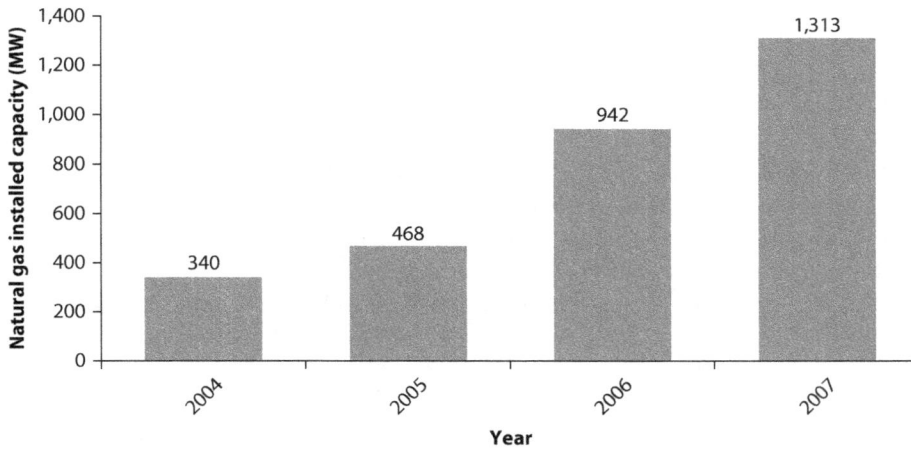

Source: World Bank 2008.

is composed of 220 and 138 kilovolt lines, with a total length of 9,771 kilometers, about 60 percent of the overall length of 16,319 kilometers of the transmission network.

Incentives to Promote Renewable Energy

In Peru, 63 percent of energy is generated from renewable sources, mainly hydro, with wind power at 0.7 percent. The share of renewables thus has fallen as the share of thermoelectric power has risen. However, renewable energies are receiving strong support from the government, motivated by anticipated higher power demand, a still low level of access in rural areas, climate change commitments, and energy security—and the government wants renewables to account for 33 percent of generation by 2021, up from less than 1 percent now, if large hydro is excluded. In May 2008, the government issued Decree 1002 establishing incentives for promoting renewable energy—which cover solar, wind, biomass, geothermal, tidal, and small hydro—but not large hydro. These incentives include:

- *Renewable energy quota.* The government established a 5 percent mandatory quota for the period 2008–13. The quota has to be updated every five years
- *Auctions.* The investor is guaranteed a fixed price during the 20 years of the contract
- *Preferential treatment.* Developers have priority access to the transmission and distribution grids
- *Tax incentives.* A program of accelerated depreciation for renewable energy projects.

Peru has dived into promoting renewables—for which there is enormous untapped potential (especially in solar and wind)—with technology-specific contract auctions for renewable energy based on targets set by a government-approved development plan (Barroso 2011). So far, the government has held two auctions (Maurer and Barroso 2011). The first call was in 2008, when the country organized an auction focused on hydropower under 20 megawatts. The government managed to cover 68 percent of the required energy for wind, biomass, and solar technologies (OSINERG), but for hydroelectric stations, only 32 percent. As a result, the government issued a second call, during which it had to adjudicate a 18 megawatts hydroelectric project. The remaining participants were disqualified due to offers with higher prices than those set by OSINERG, and quotas for biomass and hydro were not filled (figure 3.11).

For the second auction in February 2010, OSINERG awarded 26 projects to supply 500 megawatts from renewable energy over 20 years, with projects in biomass, wind, solar, and hydro under 20 megawatts. This first call was regarded as a great success by sector investors, given the certainty it provides on future cash flows for any given project. In June, OSINERG released consolidated bidding rules for a second auction for late 2010, with an expected supply of an additional 338 megawatts of hydro, as well as requirements for up to 419 and 8 gigawatt-hour per year from biomass and solar, respectively. Winning generators were awarded contracts with distribution companies (to be passed-through to regulated consumers) for up to 20 years to deliver the annual amount of energy offered at its agreed price for three years ahead (Barroso 2011). As in the Brazilian case, demand pays a fixed annual amount and collects the spot market revenue.

Figure 3.11 Peru's First Auction Did Not Fill All Quotas

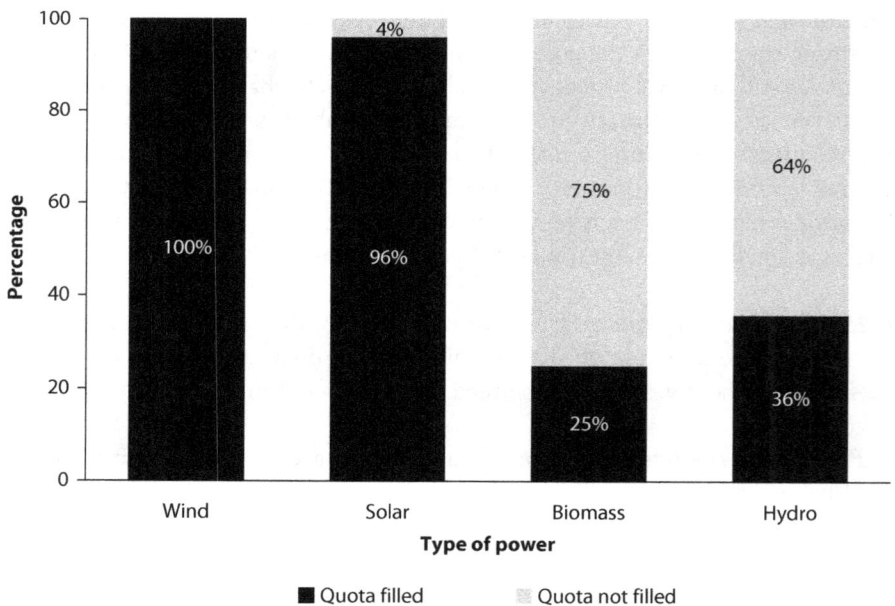

Source: Ramirez and Acosta 2010.

By 2011, eight renewable energy-based generation stations were producing electricity for the National Interconnected System (seven of them started operations in April 2010 and the eighth began in July 2010). The rest of the projects will start by the end of 2012. Out of the total energy that will be produced by the successful bidders, 30 will come from biomass, and the rest from small hydro. Renewable energy tariffs have been covering 100 percent of the costs and expected benefits of the projects, with income originating from the sale of electricity in the short-term market plus additional fees paid by consumers.

The Case of Mexico

Electricity Market Reforms

The electricity sector in Mexico is mostly state-owned. With the exception of generation, where there is 25 percent of private sector participation, the rest of the sectors are served by the state-owned company, the Federal Electricity Commission (CFE). CFE has an installed capacity of 46,686 megawatts in 218 power plants and an estimated number of 22 million consumers. CFE defines the investment program with the lowest cost for the electricity sector, with a 10 year planning horizon. It is also responsible for planning, construction, and operation of the national electric system and is subject to government regulation and supervision by the Mexican government.

Generation

Mexico's energy mix is dominated by fossil fuels (figure 3.12). In 2010, electricity generation was 241,491 gigawatt-hour, with two-thirds coming from hydrocarbons. Natural gas has been the main fuel used for producing electricity, with its share rising from 14 percent in 1998 to 48.8 percent in 2008—while the share of fossil fuel fell from 51.7 percent in 1998 to 18.3 percent in 2008.

Meanwhile, Mexico has been gradually boosting the share of renewable energies—which reached 18.01 percent in 2010. Of the country's total generation, 15.2 percent comes from hydroelectricity, 0.07 percent from wind, and 2.74 percent from geothermal.

After Mexico's debt crisis in 1994/95, it began to open up the fully state-owned power sector to private investors again, and in recent years, private sector investment in electricity has risen sharply. In 2008 the private sector, either under the form of self-provision or cogeneration, contributed, respectively, 6.7 percent and 4.5 percent of the country's total installed capacity.

Of the total private investment in electricity, more than 90 percent is foreign, and that percentage rises to close to 100 percent for foreign investment in the sector of independent producers and exporters. Private sector producers apply 11 technologies, the most used being combined cycle technology (70 percent). Within the private sector the energy mix is composed of natural gas (81 percent), other solid fossil fuels (15 percent) and renewable energies

Figure 3.12 Mexico's Energy Use Is Dominated by Fossil Fuels but Renewable Are Growing

electricity generation by source[a] (GWh)

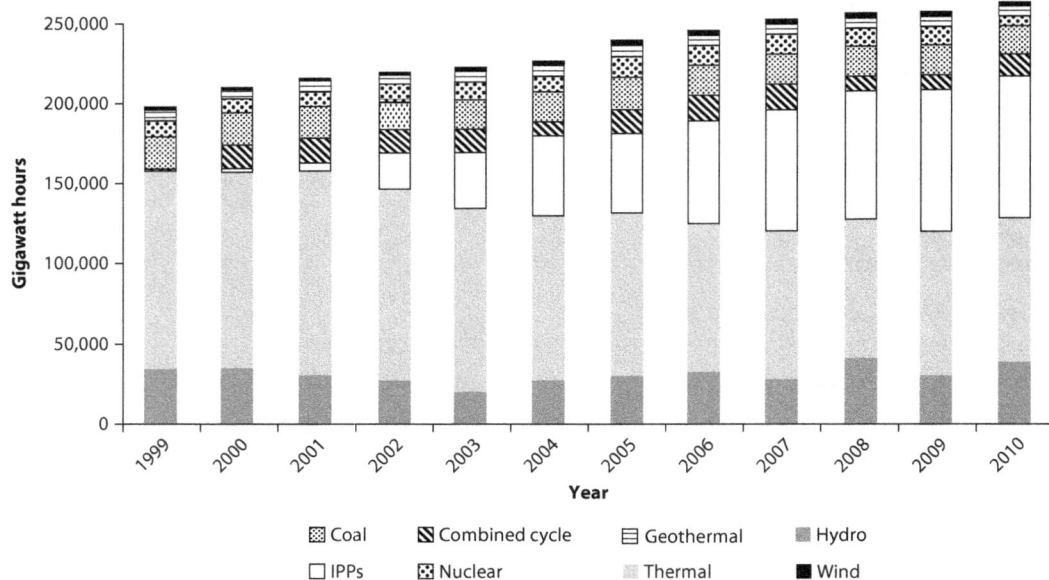

Legend:
⊠ Coal   ◪ Combined cycle   ⊟ Geothermal   ▦ Hydro
☐ IPPs   ⊠ Nuclear   ▨ Thermal   ■ Wind

Source: SENER.
a. Does not include self-generation and cogeneration.

(4 percent). Among private producers, installed capacity increased 2.8 percent with regards to 2007. Independent producers represented 59.9 percent of total installed capacity.

For regulation purposes, electricity generation is divided into two types: public service and not for public service. Public service is the generation of electricity to distribute among consumers. Not for public service is divided among (1) self-provision; (2) cogeneration (production of electricity together with thermal or another type of secondary thermal energy); (3) independent production (generation of electricity from a station with a capacity higher than 30 megawatts, destined exclusively to CFE or for export); and (4) small production (electricity sold to CFE, which is less than 30 megawatts or for export within those limits and/or electricity generated for small communities under 1 megawatts).

Electricity transmission

For Mexico, congestion in transmitting electricity poses a major challenge, amounting to an estimated loss of US$1.4 billion per year. But it also creates a potential incentive for using power generated by local markets. Some areas, such as the Yucatan peninsula, remain particularly isolated because their only links to the main national grid are small congested lines. According to Rosellon, this problem will become more severe in the near future because national demand for transmission capacity keeps growing (Rosellon 2006). The rate of capacity

Figure 3.13 Transmission Lines Are Getting Longer

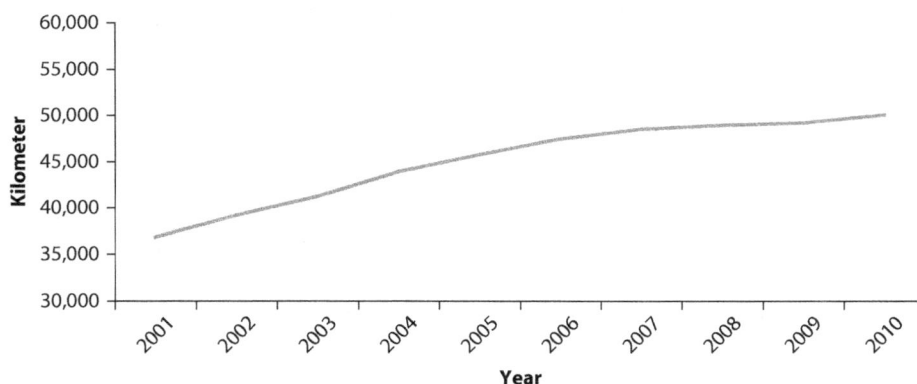

Source: SENER.

growth has ballooned over the past decade, rising from about 4 percent between 1981 and 2001 to more than 20 percent between 2002 and 2006. The length of transmission lines has shot up from around 35,000 kilometers in 2001 to 50,000 kilometers in 2010 (figure 3.13).

Transmission tariffs in Mexico are set according to the cost of service per megawatt-mile. This method provides no proper effective incentives for expanding the grid and relies instead on a subjective way of allocating costs among consumers according to their so-called presumed impact on the grid (Rosellon 2006). Using this method, charges for transmission services for tensions equal to or greater than 69 kilovolt are calculated as the maximum between "fixed costs plus variable costs" and "operation and maintenance costs." Administrative fixed costs—which are basically the long-run incremental cost of the transmission network—are then added to this amount. They are allocated among consumers of the current grid and consumers of the future expanded grid according to their impact across the entire network.

Incentives to Promote Renewable Energy

In the early 2000s, when Mexico wanted to diversify its fossil-fuel dominated fuel mix and promote the use of renewable energy, its Energy Regulatory Commission established different regulatory instruments—in the form of contracts and incentives—aimed at increasing renewable energy penetration in the system. The key ones are:

- *Interconnection contract*. This is the main instrument to regulate the terms and conditions of the interconnection between the national system, the renewable energy developer, and the electricity provider. It allows the surplus of electricity produced by licensees in a given month either to be sold to the electricity provider in that particular month or to be stored at the Energy Bank of the national electricity utility for its use or sale during the next 12 months

- *Electricity Transmission Agreement.* This was established to allow the transportation of electricity from the renewable energy source to electricity providers
- *Tax incentives.* Income tax payers who invest in electricity generation from renewable energy can deduct 100 percent of the investment as long as they operate the machinery for at least five years.

In 2008, Mexico passed the *Law for the Promotion of Renewable Energies and the Financing of Energy Transition.* The law's overriding objective is to promote the use of renewable energy for purposes other than utility services. As a result of the law, the government has also established the *National Strategy for Energy Transition and the Promotion of Sustainable Energy.*

Over the past decade, the increase of renewable energies in Mexico, especially wind technologies, has involved significant levels of private sector investment (figure 3.14). In fact, the private sector has been responsible for 76 percent of total investment in wind projects, according to Mexico's Secretary of Energy. This investment is occurring at the level of self-generation.

In 2006, Mexico implemented an "open bid" system—known as the Open Season approach—to expand its transmission grid by connecting wind energy to the national electricity system. The first agreement was between the publicly owned enterprise (the Federal Electricity Commission) and the private industry to build 145 kilometers of transmission lines from La Ventosa to the sub-station Juile. How does this new approach work? The public utility determines transmission infrastructure needs given initial private sector interest in developing wind power (both self-supply and PPA commercial schemes). A transmission plan is then presented to wind power developers to gauge their interest in reserving firm transmission capacity. After details are agreed, a final plan is prepared

Figure 3.14 Private Investors Lead the Way in Wind Power

committed wind projects in Mexico by ownership, MW

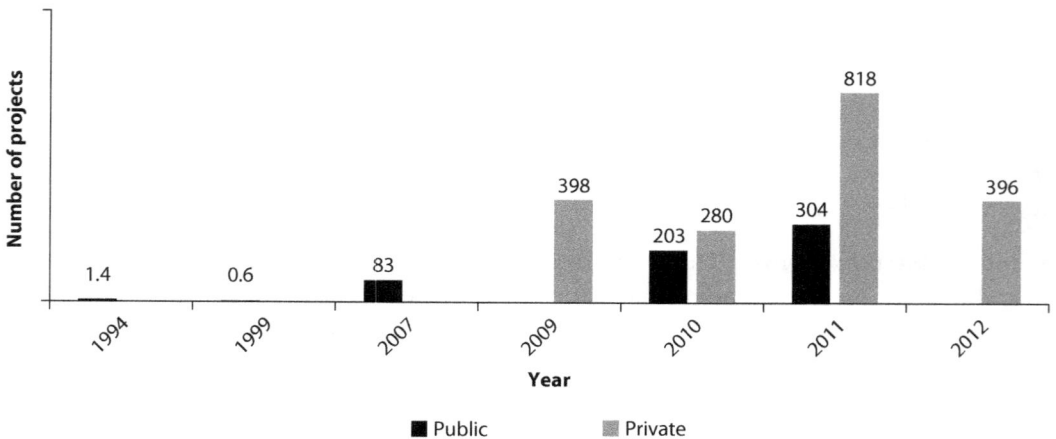

Source: SENER.

and an "open season" starts, requesting formal commitments for firm transmission capacity reservations.

Renewable energy developers must provide guarantees, in the form of letters of interests, based on the following conditions (1) 5 percent of the estimated cost of the Open Season must be paid at the same time of the presentation of the company's expression of interest, (2) 25 percent of the total cost must be paid once government authorization takes place, and (3) 100 percent must be paid one month before the beginning of the tendering process. The utility commits to building the necessary infrastructure to connect the total capacity of wind projects to the electricity grid. The open season approach "pools" transmission costs, which are shared among wind power developers (costs are not passed to customers).

The Mexican authorities consider the open season approach a success. Since its establishment in 2006, there has been an exponential growth of wind energy development, moving from almost negligible levels before then to about 250 megawatt-hour in the 2007–09 period (see figure 3.15).

In April 2010, Mexico's energy regulator (CRE) published a new methodology to calculate the transmission costs of renewable energy projects. The regulation will require the state power company CFE to charge around US$2.5–5.0 per megawatt-hour depending on the voltage, to transmit electricity from renewable and cogeneration sources on the national power system. Previously, the tariffs were not standardized and required CFE to hire an expert to conduct a study on the site. The protocol brought a lot of uncertainty to investors about what the final price would be to pay CFE for transmission. Depending on the specific conditions of each project, this new methodology could cut rates as much as 50 percent.

Figure 3.15 The "Open Season" System Is a Huge Success in Wind Power

evolution of electricity generation from wind, MWh

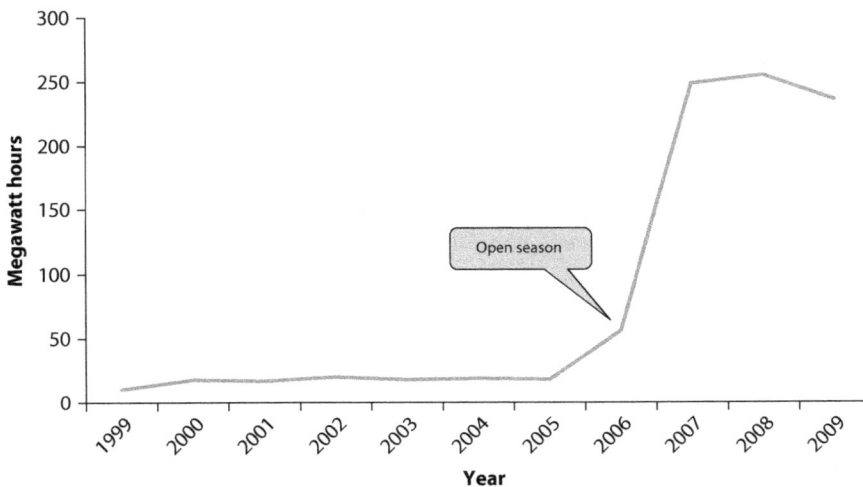

Source: SENER 2009.

Conclusions

So what lessons can we draw from case studies on China, Brazil, Peru, and Mexico? The case study evidence suggests that:

- *There is a significant trade-off between effectiveness and efficiency of alternative instruments for deploying renewables.* Feed-in tariffs tended to be quite effective but to be set on the high side, reducing incentives to cut costs and posing significant strains on already stripped national budgets. Competitive auctions, on the other hand have tended to be efficient but initially low and not always the most effective instrument
- *Countries can scale up renewables following different paths.* For Brazil, the move from feed-in tariffs to auctions enabled it to both reduce costs and deploy additional capacity. Peru followed in Brazil's path, opting for auctions instead of introducing feed-in tariffs. On the other hand, China's move from competitive tenders to feed-in tariffs allowed for discovery effects to determine the right level of prices to attract private investment in renewables
- *Private investors require technical and regulatory certainty about the availability of renewable-ready transmission resources if they are to finance investments.* The traditional reactive model of transmission regulation—developing transmission on a first-come, first-served basis—is not conducive for renewables, as it introduces extensive regulatory and technical uncertainty about whether adequate transmission will be available once the resource is generated, and transmission distances for renewables can be large. The case of China is quite telling in that the sharp increase in renewables (particularly wind) posed challenges to the stability of the transmission system. In contrast, Mexico used an open season approach, with new transmission investment decided through an agreement between the Federal Electricity Commission and private investors, which facilitated better regulatory and technical certainty.

Notes

1. Some assessments stress the limitations of the Brazilian auction system (Dutra and Menezes 2005). According to this line of argument, the Brazilian system is affected by what they call *"higher costs of reforms in developing economies"* because of a lack of trust in both government and institutional design issues.

2. *Peru, Institutional and Financial Framework for Development of Small Hydropower,* ESMAP draft report, june 2008; *Peru, Framework for Hydropower Development,* Section of Valuation of Natural Gas Alternative Uses; on-going study.

3. In the case of electricity generation, liquefied natural gas would be the economic alternative if Camisea natural gas would not be available.

4. The concession of the grid was given to Consorcio Transmantaro S.A., who strategic partner is Hydro Québec (Canada).

References

China

Cheung, K. 2011. "Integration of Renewables: Status and Challenges in China." Working Paper, Paris: International Energy Agency.

Junfeng, Li., S. Pengfei, and G. Hu. 2010. *China Wind Power Outlook*. Global Wind Energy Council (GWEC) Chinese Renewable Energy Industries Association, Global Wind Energy Council Greenpeace, Octobar 2010.

Renewable Energy Policy Network for the 21st Century. 2009. "Recommendations for Improving the Effectiveness of Renewable Energy Policies in China." http://www.ren21.net/Portals/97/documents/publications/Recommendations_for_RE_policies_in_china.pdf

Tawney, L., R. Bell, and M. Ziegler. 2011. "High Wire Act: Electricity Transmission Infrastructure and its Impact on the Renewable Energy Market". Washington, DC: World Resource Institute.

World Bank. 2010. "China's Envisaged Renewable Energy Target China Sets Solar Power Price to Boost Profits, Investment." *Bloomberg News*, August 2011. http://www.bloomberg.com/news/2011-08-01/chinese-government-sets-nationwide-solar-photovoltaic-power-on-grid-prices.html.

Brazil

ANEEL (Agencia Nacional de Electricidade). 2011. "Electricity Generation Database." ANEEL'S www.aneel.gov.br.

Dutra. J. and F. Menezes. 2005. "Lessons from the Electricity Auctions in Brazil," Electricity Journal, 18(10), 11–21. World Bank. 2008. Institutional and Financial Framework for Development of small Hydropower, ESMAP Report, http://siteresources.worldbank.org/INTPERUINSPANISH/Resources/Estudiopeguenasttidroelectricas.pdf

Empresa de Pesquisa Energética. 2011. Datasets.

Jannuzzi, G. D. M. 2004. "Power Sector Reforms in Brazil and its Impacts on Energy Efficiently and Research and Development Activities." Energy Discussion Paper No. 2.62-01/04, International Energy Initiative, Latin American Office, Sâo Paulo, Brazil.

Maurer, L., and L. Barroso. 2011. "Electricity Auctions: An Overview of Efficient Practices." World Bank and ESMAP. Washington, DC: World Bank.

Serrato, E. 2008. "Electricity Transmission Sector in Brazil: Analysis of the Auctions' Results and the Public and the Private Firms' Costs." Institute of Brazilian Issues. Washington, DC: George Washington University.

Mexico

Rosellón, J. and H. Weight. 2011. "A Dynamic Incentive Mechanism for Transmission Expansion in Electricity Networks: Theory, Modeling, Application" *Energy Journal*, vol. 32, n. 4.

Peru

Ramirez, R., and E. Acosta. 2010. "Análisis Económico de la Subasta de Electricidad con Energías Renovables." Presentation at the 5th Economic Regulation Conference of Iberoamerica, Lima. November 24, 2010.

How the Financial Crisis Affected Various Developing Countries

Table A.1 Impact of the Financial Crisis on Financing and Investment in the Power Sector of 18 Developing Countries

	Power sector structure	*Financial crisis impact*	*Financing sources*	*Investment plan*	*Funding gap*
		South Asia			
India	Generating capacity ownership[a]: 52.5% State government 34% Central government 13.5% Private	No substantial impact on electric power infrastructure investments. The availability of credit shifted away from private sector projects towards state sector projects.	Government-owned entities can borrow at competitive rates through the bank credit route or the bond finance route. Commercial banks preferred to extend credit to public sector entities over private sector projects during the financial crisis.	Ambitious plans to augment electricity supply and access.	—
Pakistan	Current power deficit is 4–5 GW.	Continues to rely on foreign inflows from the IMF and the US for budgetary support and solvency. IPPs were delayed due to difficulties in obtaining financing. Government resorted to rental power plants.	Unwillingness of foreign investors to finance power projects. Overexposure of domestic banks to the power sector hinders further investment.	*Vision 2020 Program:* Add 20 GW by 2020 at an estimated cost of over US$32 billion, with 45% (US$15 billion) financed by private sources.	Up to US$32 billion until 2020 if private and state funding unavailable

(table continues on next page)

Table A.1 Impact of the Financial Crisis on Financing and Investment in the Power Sector of 18 Developing Countries (continued)

	Power sector structure	Financial crisis impact	Financing sources	Investment plan	Funding gap
Bangladesh	Absence of private investment since 2002. Over 50% of the population does not have access to electricity. Power deficit of 2 GW.	Economy proved to be very resilient to the fallout from the financial crisis. However, project syndication markets have dried up.	Domestic financing is available for power projects, however projects in excess of US$70–100 million are difficult to finance locally. Larger IPPS required international finance and support from multilaterals.	The main challenge for Bangladesh is to obtain senior debt with tenors greater than 15 years, which requires risk mitigating instruments. Multilateral financial institutions could provide support.	—
			East Asia and Pacific		
Vietnam	Characterized by state owned enterprises (SOE) Vietnam Electricity Group (EVN) is the main power utility. 80% of the power sector is publicly owned.	In 2009, EVN had a financing cap of US$175 million for three substantially complete projects, and an additional funding shortfall through 2010 of US$612 million.	Rural electrification is funded by the government, and through grants or concessional loans from bilaterals and multilaterals. Local banks are still willing to lend to projects, but are limited by the regulatory lending limit of 15% of each bank's equity per borrower.	Power Development Master Plan Six: US$4 billion/year in 2011–15, of which 75% is for generation. Capacity addition of 3.75 GW is required to restore reserve margins.	—
Indonesia	Electricity demand is projected to triple by 2020. The power sector is predominantly publicly owned.	Slowdown in power sector investment: of the 62 IPPs representing about 9 GW of capacity, 31 projects in preparation are still trying to reach financial closure with funding needs of US$3.6 billion.	Foreign banks are willing to fund IPPs only with government guarantees. Local banks have liquidity and are still willing to lend but only in local currency.	*10 GW Program to 2015* Required investment in generation, transmission, and distribution is US$41.4 billion from 2006 to 2015, of which 68% will be undertaken by the main public utility.	US$5 billion for the 10 GW program. US$3.6 billion for current projects trying to reach financial closure.
Philippines	Power sector reform in 2004 Separation of generation and transmission	The sale of publicly owned generation assets was stalled due to the financial crisis.	Local banks are able and willing to lend to IPP developers at rates competitive with foreign banks,	—	—

(table continues on next page)

Table A.1 Impact of the Financial Crisis on Financing and Investment in the Power Sector of 18 Developing Countries (continued)

	Power sector structure	Financial crisis impact	Financing sources	Investment plan	Funding gap
	By the end of 2008, 48% of capacity was privatized Wholesale competitive sport market started in Luzon in 2006.	—	but are hampered by single borrower credit limits for existing owners of generation assets. ECA and bilateral funding is available.	—	—
Middle East and North Africa					
Morocco	Private generators account for 68% of electricity production. Transmission remains a state monopoly.	No project has been cancelled due to the financial crisis, but some have experienced delays.	Donors, local commercial banks, and ECAs provide financing to the power sector. Morocco is still an attractive market for international banks.	Cumulative investment in the power sector would amount to US$10 billion from 2009 to 2015.	None expected.
Tunisia	Public utility generates 70% of electricity supply, and has a monopoly over transmission and distribution. Only two IPPS: 470 MW combined cycle gas turbine plant (2002) and 30 MW gas turbine (2003).	The overall cost of financing has increased.	The public utility relies heavily on subsidies, as tariffs are far from covering costs. IFIs, ECAs, and Arab funds provide financing. Local banks also provide financing only up to seven years.	Several planned mega-projects will add 1.6 GW of capacity from 2011 to 2016.	None expected.
Egypt	Public utility is the single buyer of electricity. Private generators accounted for only 10% of electricity supply in 2008. Unmet peak load demand.	The crisis stifled the momentum for private sector engagement in the power sector. However, impact of the crisis has been limited.	Financing of new investment in the next five years will be a challenge, since the public sector power companies are highly indebted. IFIs and ECAs will play an important role in financing, but local banks are also active.	Over 11 GW of additional generating capacity and investment in transmission and distribution are planned over the next seven years at a cost of US$21.3 billion. Only US$1.5 billion will be funded by the private sector.	—
Jordan	First privately-owned power company was established in the 1930s. The 2000s saw further privatization.	No major project cancellation to date.	Local and offshore debt financing are available. Commercial debt financing has increased along with more private sector participation in the sector.	Planned investment of US$3 billion from 2010 to 2014. More than 70% of the investment is to come from the private sector.	None expected.

(table continues on next page)

Table A.1 Impact of the Financial Crisis on Financing and Investment in the Power Sector of 18 Developing Countries (continued)

	Power sector structure	Financial crisis impact	Financing sources	Investment plan	Funding gap
		Eastern Europe and Central Asia			
Ukraine	Unbundled, single-buyer wholesale market Assets in need of significant rehabilitation, but tariffs do not cover full costs of CAPEX needs	8.7% drop in demand in 2009 delayed onset of supply gap from 2015 to 2017 or 2019. Impact of crisis was worsened by Government intervention • Requirement to buy coal from state mines drastically worsened financial performance of TPPs • Moratorium on tariff increase led to worsened financial results of DistCos	Future involvement of commercial lenders now less likely because of how the financial crisis and government intervention have affected financial performance of utilities IFIs and bilateral donors remain primary source of long-term lending to the sector	US$37.65 billion needed in 2009–12, of which 80% for generation assets.	US$30.83 billion from 2009 to 2012
Romania	1% of generation and 38% of distribution are privately owned.	Financial crisis affected economy through large drop in GDP, decline in energy-intensive industries, and tightening of fiscal space. Power companies have made OPEX cuts in employment and procurement of goods and services to try to balance budgets.	Cost of financing—even with state guarantee—has become too high for most power companies; Many banks now only willing to make new loans with 3rd party guarantee, ideally from IFIs. Restructuring of the generation sector has delayed critical investments in environmental rehabilitation and new generation capacity.	80% of thermal power plants exceed design life, most require environmental upgrades. Gap in meeting reserve margins emerges in 2013 increasing to 4,340 MW by 2017. Romania's power sector requires significant investment in rehabilitation, environmental upgrades and renewable energy to comply with EU regulations	Unknown
Serbia	100% state owned power sector was unbundled in 2005.	End-user tariffs are low compared to other countries in the region; Planned tariff increase in 2009 postponed as a result of financial crisis.	Commercial financing not source of financing in past; not likely in future unless financial performance improves	Investment Plant 2009–15 Environmental upgrade of thermal power plants: US$1.039 billion	US$3.341–6.75 billion from 2009 to 2015

(table continues on next page)

Table A.1 Impact of the Financial Crisis on Financing and Investment in the Power Sector of 18 Developing Countries (continued)

	Power sector structure	Financial crisis impact	Financing sources	Investment plan	Funding gap
	Serbian power sector is characterized by aging assets, inefficient consumption and production, and below-cost recovery tariffs.	Consumption decreased in 2009, but generation increased as a result of large increase in exports.	Donors primary source of financing for sector in past; Future financing increasingly focused on EE, RE and metering.	Construction of new capacity: US$6.428 billion Transmission: US$524 million Distribution: US$1.058 billion	
Kyrgyz Republic	State-owned vertically integrated Kyrgyzenergo unbundled in 2001. The public sector owns 93% of generation, distribution, and transmission facilities. 20% of transmission lines are older than 40 years. Generation mix: 90% hydro, 10% thermal	Kyrgyz Republic felt the effects of the financial crisis indirectly through Kazakhstan and Russia, as trade fell 20% in 2009 and remittances declined. Consumption fell in 2008 and 2009 as a result of power curtailments during winter months (due to low water levels at the Toktogul reservoir).	Multilateral donors are reluctant to make large investments in sector because of lack of transparency, however, bilateral aid—especially from China—expected to increase. Commercial financing not a source of long-term financing in past and not likely to be in the future because companies struggling to service concessional debt.	Short-Term Energy Sector Development Strategy for 2009–12: Secured US$1.022 billion of US$8.146 billion needed for thermal power plant capital expenditures	US$7.124 billion from 2009 to 2012
Armenia	The sector is fully unbundled, with the public utility controlling the transmission network and acting as the single buyer of electricity. The private sector owns 52% of generation and 100% of distribution assets.	Generating companies failed to recover full costs because of the currency devaluation in 2009 and the drop in demand. Operating expenditures increased because of rising fuel costs and the currency devaluation. Most short-term investments have financing, but medium-term projects still need funding.	Multilateral and bilateral aid has been primary source of financing for power sector in past, but currency depreciation and higher lending rates have made borrowing more difficult Commercial banks not traditionally a large source of financing for most sector entities but financial crisis has tightened lending terms: higher rates, stricter collateral requirements Improving financial performance of power sector utilities needed to attract both concessional and commercial financing	520 km of transmission lines in need of urgent rehabilitation at a cost of US$80–100 million 600 MW supply gap will emerge when nuclear plant retires in 2017.	US$360.5 million for generation assets 2009–13

(table continues on next page)

Table A.1 Impact of the Financial Crisis on Financing and Investment in the Power Sector of 18 Developing Countries *(continued)*

	Power sector structure	*Financial crisis impact*	*Financing sources*	*Investment plan*	*Funding gap*
	Latin America and the Caribbean				
Colombia	Power sector reform in early 1990s: 32% of market is deregulated wholesale market 80% hydropower Private sector controls 55% of generation, 4% of transmission, 52% of distribution	Thus far, with the exception of one large hydroelectric project, generation companies have been able to arrange financing to meet construction schedules, and in most cases do not envisage difficulties in funding the projects planned for 2010 and 2011.	New projects: Securing funding for the 9 new generation projects awarded in 2008 is a major concern now. Access to syndicated loans in the international capital market is limited and expensive. The government no longer provides sovereign guarantees to back IFI´s loans to state-owned enterprises. Existing projects: In 2009, the domestic bond market liquidity was high. Existing generators have good credit ratings in the domestic market, which will facilitate balance sheet financing.	In 2008, plan for 9 new generation plants with an installed capacity of about 3,400 MW, sufficient to meet projected demand until 2017 at a cost of US$7 billion.	None expected.
Peru	Power sector reform in early 1990s Private sector controls 71% of generation 100% of transmission 69% of distribution	Positive impact: A high risk of an energy supply crisis in 2009 was averted when the high demand growth almost stopped However the crisis also had a negative, but not critical, impact on the financing of new investments in the power sector	Domestic capital, though tight at the end of 2008, increased its liquidity and became an important source of financing for new generation projects in 2009. Access to the international capital market was difficult. The IFC is considering financing various renewable energy projects.	Development of about 2,700 MW in thermoelectric plants, mostly combined cycle gas turbines, and 1,100 MW in renewable generation.	None expected.

(table continues on next page)

Table A.1 Impact of the Financial Crisis on Financing and Investment in the Power Sector of 18 Developing Countries *(continued)*

	Power sector structure	Financial crisis impact	Financing sources	Investment plan	Funding gap
Jamaica	95% of installed capacity is based on diesel and Heavy Fuel Oil Electricity tariffs are among the highest in the Western Hemisphere at USc24/kWh. Despite its limited size (about 1,200 MW installed capacity), the structure of the power sector is complex and involves a large number of institutions.	Bond rating of Jamaican bonds downgraded by two notches in November 2009, increased again after IMF agreement in Feb 2010. Capacity shortage possible by 2014 The non-wind renewable energy program and the energy efficiency program have been scaled down from US$50 million to US$20 million over 2010–17. In addition, the replacement of high cost and low efficiency units will be deferred by two to three years.	Donor financing from IDB and PetroCaribe decreased significantly. Bilateral and multilateral donors	Heavy fuel oil per gas fired capacity: 150 MW and 200 MW plants to be completed in 2015, 150 MW plant to be completed in 2017 Wind plant capacity at US$240 million by 2017 on target, but financing not yet secured Non-wind renewables: US$132 million funding gap	US$132 million for non-wind renewables and energy efficiency

Sources: World Bank 2010a, 2010b; ESMAP 2010a, 2010b, 2010c, 2010d, 2010f.
Note: IFC = International Finance Corporation, IMF = International Monetary Fund, IDB = Inter-American Development Bank; — = not available.
a. Government of India 2010.

Climate Change Projections for Investments Needs Vary Greatly

Table B.1 Review of Estimates for Additional Mitigation and Adaptation Investment Needs

Source of estimate	Projected investment need	Sectors	Potential sources	Source of estimate	Projected investment need	Sectors	Potential sources
Mitigation—macro level estimates				*Adaptation—macro level estimates*			
Bottom-up Approaches				*Bottom-up Approaches*			
Stern Review (2007)	**586–2,320** annually between 2010 and 2050	Specific	Not specifically named	*UNFCCC (2007)*	**49–171** (28–67 non-OECD) annually by 2030	Specific	Named
IEA ETP (2008)	**400–1,100** annually through 2050	Specific	Not specifically named	*Parry (2009) report based on UNFCCC*	UNFCCC 2007 estimates up to **8 times higher**	Specific	Not specifically named
McKinsey & Company (2009)	**400** (208 non-OECD) annually through 2015	Economy-wide	Not specifically named	*Project Catalyst (2009)*	**13–25** annually between 2010 and 2020	Specific	Named
	1,025 (661 non-OECD) annually between 2015 and 2030	—	—				
Top-down Approaches				*Top-down Approaches*			
UNFCCC (2007)	**200–210** annually by/in 2030	Specific	Named	*WBG Clean Energy Framework (2006)*	**9–41** annually between 2010 and 2015	Economy-wide	Named
OECD Environmental Outlook (2008)	**170–9,446** annually between 2010 and 2050	Economy-wide	Not specifically named	*Stern Review (2007)*	**4–37** annually between 2010 and 2015	Economy-wide	Not specifically named

(table continues on next page)

Table B.1 Review of Estimates for Additional Mitigation and Adaptation Investment Needs *(continued)*

Source of estimate	Projected investment need	Sectors	Potential sources	Source of estimate	Projected investment need	Sectors	Potential sources
OECD Burniaux et al. (2009)	**393–12,205** annually between 2012 and 2050 w/ modest over-shooting	Economy-wide	Not specifically named	**UNDP (2008)**	**86–109** annually between 2010 and 2015	Economy-wide	Not specifically named
	754—22,913 annually between 2012 and 2050 w/o modest over-shooting	—	—				
				Oxfam (2008)	**>50** annually between 2010 and 2015	Economy-wide	Not specifically named
				EACC World Bank (2009)	**75–100** annually between 2010 and 2050	Specific	Not specifically named
	Hybrid approaches				*Hybrid approaches*		
IPCC (2007)	**204–11,289** annually between 2010 and 2050	Economy-wide	Not specifically named	**IPCC (2007)**	No new estimates but high benefit cost ratio for adaptation	—	Not specifically named
PIK (2009)	**–0.5 to –2.5%** of annual global GDP between 2000 and 2100	Economy-wide	Not specifically named				

Additional investment needs regarding Mitigation and Adaptation costs estimates, unless otherwise stated in 2005US$ billion pa, at E = 1.25US$ per Euro where applicable. If case estimates were given as % of global GDP or annual average GDP growth, total numbers were based on WB WDI 2009 data setting global GDP in 2007 at 52,850.4 2005US$ billion and an assumed average global GDP growth of 3.5% between 2010 and 2050 unless otherwise stated.

Note: — = not available.

Source of estimate	Projected investment need	Sectors	Methodology applied	Comments on methodology	Potential sources of investments named
			1. Mitigation—macro level estimates		
			1.1 Bottom-up approaches		
Stern Review (2007)	−1.0% to 3.5% of annual GDP, with average estimate of 1% of GDP/year through 2050 ⇒ **586–2,320** annually between 2010 and 2050	Electricity generation; transport and industry	Average cost of mitigation per ton of carbon is constructed by calculating the cost of each technology weighted by the assumed take-up, and comparing this with the emissions reductions achieved by these technologies against fossil-fuel alternatives. For each technology, assumptions are made on plausible rates of uptake over time though there might be problems with regard to increasing marginal cost. Assumptions are also made on the potential for energy-efficiency improvements. These assumptions are then used to calculate an average cost of mitigation. The costs of mitigation are expected to decline by half over the next 20 years, and then by a further third by 2050.	Rather long-term estimates may become problematic, as for example, although average costs of each technology may fall, marginal costs are likely to be on a rising trajectory through time.	Not specifically named
IEA Energy Technology Perspective (2008)	400–1,100 annual average through 2050	Power sector (excluding transmission and distribution)	In order to estimate mitigation costs, the study draws upon a global ***Marginal Abatement Cost Curve*** for 2050, which was developed using current cost data and respective cost projections. The curve is then applied to different scenarios developed under IEA's World Energy Model for the WEO 2007.	Some general problems with the marginal abatement cost curve consist in the fact that it does not really represent marginal cost since oil and gas prices are assumed to be static whereas they fluctuate in the respective scenarios; it is further difficult to come up with a single cost figure for options that affect capital stock, a cost range would be much more appropriate but, depending on the number of assumptions used, might be too wide in order to yield an acceptable overall investment estimate.	Not specifically named

(table continues on next page)

Table B.1 Review of Estimates for Additional Mitigation and Adaptation Investment Needs *(continued)*

Source of estimate	Projected investment need	Sectors	Methodology applied	Comments on methodology	Potential sources of investments named
McKinsey & Company (2009)	400 (208 non–OECD) annually through 2015 1,025 (661 non–OECD) annually between 2015 and 2030	Economy-wide	McKinsey's **Global GHG Abatement Cost Curve** shall serve as a basis for discussion about what mitigation levers exist; how to compare mitigation opportunities and costs between countries and sectors; and how to discuss what incentives to put in place. All costs are estimated on the basis of current cost and estimated projections on the basis of models, expert views and educated extrapolation using a predefined mitigation cost formula (see Annex III of McKinsey 2009).	Some general problems with the marginal abatement cost curve consist in the fact that it does not really represent marginal cost since oil and gas prices are assumed to be static whereas they fluctuate in the respective scenarios; it is further difficult to come up with a single cost figure for options that affect capital stock, a cost range would be much more appropriate but, depending on the number of assumptions used, might be too wide in order to yield an acceptable overall investment estimate as macroeconomic variables might have a high impact on results and error margins. Serves more as a toolbox of cost estimates for different technologies in individual countries and sectors than as a useful global estimate.	Not specifically named
			1.2 Top-down approaches		
UNFCCC (2007)	200–210 annually by/ in 2030	Energy supply; industry; buildings; transportation; waste; agriculture; forestry and R&D.	The study projects relevant investment (initial capital spending for physical assets) and financial (expenditures related to mitigation) flows by sector for a reference as well as a mitigation scenario on the basis of the 2006 IEA WEO and data provided by EPA and IPCC (among else from the IIASA). Total investment flows are given as domestic gross fixed capital formation (hence overall domestic investments plus ODA, FDI and public and private international debt).	Projections of future investment flows are available by economic sector but not by source. Projections of future FDI, public and private international debt and ODA are also not available. Hence investment needs or future investment flows were assessed on the basis of current sources of investment for the sector.	Study states that a substantial part of projected investment needs can be covered with currently available sources assuming appropriate policies and incentives, but there is still need for additional external sources.

(table continues on next page)

Table B.1 Review of Estimates for Additional Mitigation and Adaptation Investment Needs *(continued)*

Source of estimate	Sectors	Projected investment need	Methodology applied	Comments on methodology	Potential sources of investments named
OECD Environmental Outlook (2008)	Economy-wide	Reduction in average annual global GDP growth of about 0.1% between 2010 and 2050 ⇒ **170–9,446** annually between 2010 and 2050	Analysis upon the basis of a new version of the OECD/World Bank JOBS/Linkages model—ENV-Linkages, which serves as a global general equilibrium model containing 26 sectors and 34 world regions, capable of providing economic projections for multiple time periods. Overall mitigation cost estimate is based upon a scenario of a 450 ppm CO2eq stabilization pathway.	The modeling used draws upon a very wide basis of data and assumptions and does therefore not come up with a very specific estimate for mitigation investment needs.	Not specifically named
OECD Burniaux et al. (2009)	Economy-wide	4.75% of global GDP in 2050 under a GHG concentration stabilized at 550 ppm-baseline scenario with modest overshooting—which equals lowering average annual world GDP growth between 2012 and 2050 by 0.13% from about 3.5% to 3.37% **(by 393–12,205 annually).** Without overshooting cost would be 9% of global GDP *in 2050*— equal to lowering average annual world GDP growth between 2012 and 2050 by 0.25% from about 3.5% to 3.25% **(by 754–22,913 annually).**	The estimates builds upon a model which assumes a global price on carbon, whereby the cost of abating one ton of carbon is equalized across all countries, industries and GHGs in order to provide lower bound estimates of aggregate emission reduction costs. Study mentions that cost estimates could be lowered if energy subsidies were to be removed; if barriers to imports of climate-friendly goods and services were to be lifted; if low-cost forestry CO_2 mitigation potential were to be mobilized; and if major new low-carbon technologies emerged as a result of mitigation policies.	Model provides a useful benchmark against which to assess the costs and emissions reduction potential of alternative policy options. However the above cost estimates are optimistic in that they assume smooth adjustment to a global price-based policy approach. In addition one would have to take into account that even in a benchmark scenario, mitigation costs vary significantly depending on the nature, horizon, and stringency of the target, as well as on the path towards it, which could involve temporarily overshooting long-term concentration targets.	Not specifically named

(table continues on next page)

Table B.1 Review of Estimates for Additional Mitigation and Adaptation Investment Needs *(continued)*

Source of estimate	Projected investment need	Sectors	Methodology applied	Comments on methodology	Potential sources of investments named
			1.3 Hybrid approaches		
IPCC (2007)	–5,5% to +1% of annual GDP by 2050 Or reduction in average annual global GDP growth by 0.12% between 2010 and 2050 (**by 204–11,289 annually**).	Economy-wide	—	Huge scope in report's estimated mitigation cost is due to varying assumptions about future socio-economic growth, technological change and consumption patterns. Especially developments regarding technology diffusion, long-term technology performance and cost-efficiency improvements can have a huge impact on overall investment needs/cost of mitigation estimates.	Not specifically named
Potsdam Institute for Climate Impact Research (PIK) (2009)	–0.5 to –2.5% of annual global GDP in between 2000 and 2100	Economy-wide	Estimates based on two optimal growth models MERGE-ETL and REMIND-R, which are hybrid models with a top-down macroeconomic model and a bottom-up energy system model. Both are optimal growth models where a social planner with perfect foresight maximizes global welfare over a given period. Solved at equilibrium, these optimization models yield least-cost energy systems under a set of constraints.	Estimates produced by the two theoretical models have a rather large scope and are quite sensitive to a broad variety of assumptions and conditions.	Not specifically named
			2. Adaptation—macro level estimates		
			2.1 Bottom-up approaches		
UNFCCC (2007)	49–171 (28–67 non OECD) annually by 2030	Agriculture, forestry and fisheries; water supply; human health; coastal zones; infrastructure	In-depth costing of specific adaptations in water, health and coastal zones based on IPCC and (in the case of health) WHO data by 2030. Less detailed costing for agriculture, infrastructure, forestry and fisheries based on OECD model corresponding to	Clear representation of adaptation activities and how they are priced. But estimates were made using different assumptions and models for different sectors; hence the analysis of certain sectors (e.g. water and coastal zones) is based	Study states that a substantial part of projected investment needs can be covered with currently available

(table continues on next page)

Table B.1 Review of Estimates for Additional Mitigation and Adaptation Investment Needs (continued)

Source of estimate	Projected investment need	Sectors	Methodology applied	Comments on methodology	Potential sources of investments named
			IEA WEO 2006 scenario. In all cases there is a clear representation of adaptation activities that are priced. Cost for infrastructure investments account for 41 billion of the 67 billion upper bound estimate, though this number was not specifically derived but relies on Stern Review's assumption that adaptation costs will amount to 5–20% of total development finance investment flows in this field.	on more in-depth data and studies than other reports. Estimates are based on assumed percentages of what adaptation might cost, which are then applied to very large numbers of baseline investments to yield adaptation costs. There is further the danger of potential double counting as for example infrastructure overlaps with other sectors as well as undercounting, due to the narrow scope of impacts and adaptations that have been considered.	sources assuming appropriate policies and incentives, but there is still need for additional external sources, especially in low-income countries.
Parry (2009) report based on UNFCCC	UNFCCC 2007 estimates likely to be 2–3 times higher for sectors included and several times higher (up to 8 times) if all affected sectors are to be included and fully covered.	Agriculture, forestry and fisheries; water supply; human health; coastal zones; infrastructure	Report names three main reasons for under-estimation in the UNFCCC report (1) some sectors have not been included in an assessment of cost; (2) some of included sectors have only been partially covered; and (3) the additional costs of adaptation have sometimes been calculated as "climate mark-ups" against low levels of assumed investment. According to the report residual damages also need to be evaluated and reported because not all damages can be avoided due to technical and economic constraints.	According to Parry *et al.* there is an urgent need for more detailed assessments of adaptation costs. The authors recommend pursuing more robust studies of adaptation cost based upon case studies that cover a wide range of places and sectors, and support top-down analyses. They refer to McKinsey 2009 (by then still upcoming).	Not specifically named
Project Catalyst (2009)	81–125 average annual overall investment needs between 2010 and 2020 of which 13–25 annually for adaptation	Forestry; Technology; Waste; Transport; Buildings; Agriculture; Industry; Power.	Based upon the McKinsey Global GHG Abatement Cost Curve (see above under 1.1.), Project Catalyst estimates that developing countries will need around 81–125 billion of incremental cost financing flows *on average*, which are likely to ramp up over time with lower requirements in early years. These investment needs	Uses McKinsey's (2009) marginal abatement cost curve estimates for different technologies in individual countries and sectors as a basis to come up with a useful global estimate of investment needs and provides a sensitivity analysis of the potential impact of macroeconomic variables.	Potential sources of funding should include (1) Direct carbon markets; (2) Carbon market interventions; (3) ETS auction revenue; and (4) other public

(table continues on next page)

Table B.1 Review of Estimates for Additional Mitigation and Adaptation Investment Needs *(continued)*

Source of estimate	Projected investment need	Sectors	Methodology applied	Comments on methodology	Potential sources of investments named
			consist of incremental costs for abatement (adjusted at a 10% discount rate to meet higher financing rates in developing countries), transaction costs of US$1–6/ ton, and US$6 billion to support deployment of higher cost abatement technology (e.g., solar and CCS). The study has further defined certain sensitivities which might affect overall investment needs and has come up with a sensitivity analysis that gives a broader range of potential investment needs (from 50 as a lower bound in the low case to 162 as the upper bound in the high case).		and international finance sources; that could be raised from (a) international maritime and aviation levies; (b) concessional debt; and (c) direct public fiscal revenues.
			2.2 Top-down approaches		
WBG Clean Energy Framework (2006)	9–41 annually between 2010 and 2015	Not specified— presumably all sectors where ODA, FDI, and GDI are directed	The study looks at the magnitude of "climate sensitive shares" of overall development finance flows in developing countries. These are estimated as being 40% of US$100 billion in ODA; 10% of US$160 billion in FDI and 2–10% of US$1.500 billion in GDI. Adaptation costs would amount to between 10% and 20% of the respective financial shares. The climate exposed share of ODA draws upon previous studies by the World Bank and OECD, the shares for FDI and GDI have been assumed upon no prior underlying analyses.	Assumption for climate exposed share of GDI is critical due to the sheer magnitude of the underlying assumption of overall GDI—hence any modification on the climate exposed share of GDI would significantly alter the final total costs of adaptation. Currently probably not sufficient analytical data available to estimate the respective "climate sensitive shares" shares and the adaptation cost share. Study further on does not quantify the benefits of adaptation investments	Three main sources of funding are identified: internal cash generation; private financing and public finding. Depending on the overall state of development of the economy and the viability of the sectors the following shares are allotted to each source under different scenarios assuming that economies

(table continues on next page)

Table B.1 Review of Estimates for Additional Mitigation and Adaptation Investment Needs (continued)

Source of estimate	Projected investment need	Sectors	Methodology applied	Comments on methodology	Potential sources of investments named
					promoting sector reform and viable tariffs while ultimately show a larger share of private sector finance– current policies case (40% | 22% | 38%)—Improved policies case (45% 30% | 25%)—sound commercial policies case (49% | 40% | 11%).
Stern Review (2007)	4–37 annually between 2010 and 2015	Not specified— presumably all sectors where ODA, FDI, and GDI are directed	**Based upon the updated WBG 2006 adaptation cost numbers**, based upon the same assumed magnitude of "climate sensitive shares" of overall development finance flows in developing countries (40% of US$100 billion in ODA; 10% of US$160 billion in FDI and 2–10% of US$1.500 billion in GDI). Contrary to the World Bank the Stern Review assumes that adaptation would cost 5–20% of the respective financial flows	Adoption of World Bank's assumptions on shares of financial flows subject to climate risk as well as newly adopted adaptation cost range are not discussed in detail. Again as with WBG 2006 probably not sufficient analytical data available to estimate respective "climate sensitive shares" shares and the adaptation cost share.	Not specifically named

(table continues on next page)

Table B.1 Review of Estimates for Additional Mitigation and Adaptation Investment Needs *(continued)*

Source of estimate	Projected investment need	Sectors	Methodology applied	Comments on methodology	Potential sources of investments named
UNDP (2008)	86–109 annually between 2010 and 2015	Unspecified—all sectors affected by ODA, FDI or GDI interventions	**Based upon the updated WBG 2006 adaptation cost numbers**, plus cost of adapting PRSPs and strengthening disaster response. UNDP assumes that adaptation will cost between 5% and 20% of total development finance flows.	Again probably not sufficient analytical data available to estimate respective "climate sensitive shares" shares and the adaptation cost share. Some inconsistencies regarding numbers. If reports low range of necessary climate proofing investments is taken into account the lower bound estimate should be 47 instead of 86 billion.	Not specifically named
Oxfam (2008)	>50 annually between 2010 and 2015	Unspecified—apparently all sectors affected by ODA, FDI, GDI and NGO interventions	**Based upon the World Bank's (2006) adaptation cost numbers** plus cost of immediate adaptation needs formulated in individual National Adaptation Plans of Action and NGO community-level projects.	Again probably not sufficient analytical data available to estimate respective "climate sensitive shares" shares and the adaptation cost share. Potentially some double counting as community-level actions might be financed by ODA and hence already been accounted for. In addition the report extrapolates costs for National Adaptation Plans and community-level projects from a small number of point estimates to the global scale.	Not specifically named
EACC World Bank (2009)	75–100 annually between 2010 and 2050	Agriculture; Forestry; Fisheries; Infrastructure *(broken down into transport, energy, water and sanitation, communications and urban and social*	The study first crafted development baselines for each sector using GDP and population forecasts for 2010–50, thereby establishing growth paths for each sector in the absence of climate change. Then two climate scenarios were chosen to capture as large as possible a range of model predictions yielding extremes of dry and wet climate projections. The	The study's adaptation estimate is likely to be higher than the UNFCCC due to the study's more comprehensive sector coverage, as well as increases in the adaptation investment needs estimates for several sectors, especially coastal zone management and water supply and flood protection. The EACC study's estimate for infrastructure costs of adaptation falls in	Not specifically named

(table continues on next page)

Table B.1 Review of Estimates for Additional Mitigation and Adaptation Investment Needs *(continued)*

Source of estimate	Projected investment need	Sectors	Methodology applied	Comments on methodology	Potential sources of investments named
		infrastructure); Water Resources; Coastal Zones; Health; Ecosystem Services; Cross-Sectors: Extreme Weather Events; and Social Protection	results were then used to predict the impacts of changes in climate on various economic activities, on people's behavior, on environmental conditions, and on physical capital. Lastly adaptation costs were estimated by major economic sector.	the middle of the UNFCCC range, the one for health is the only one that is actually lower than in the UNFCCC study. The study looked only at additional public sector costs imposed by climate change, not the costs incurred by individuals and private agents. Similarly, the study generally opted for hard adaptation measures that require an engineering response rather than an institutional or behavioral response. "Soft" adaptation measures, as they are called by the authors, often can be more effective and can avoid the need for more expensive physical investment, but according to the authors unclear whether effective institutions and community-level collective action will exist in a given setting. While incorporating private adaptation would increase cost estimates, including "soft" measures could potentially decrease them.	
IPCC (2007)	No new estimates but high benefit cost ratio for adaptation	—	*"Costs of adaptation are not fully understood, partly because effective adaptation measures are highly dependent on specific geographical and climate risk factors as well as institutional, political and financial constraints"* (IPCC 2007, 73)	—	Not specifically named

Note: — = not available.

Methodology

Our study aims to identify the key factors affecting the private investor's decision to enter the market of generation, transmission and distribution and the amount of investment sunk in each market segment.

The analysis of the key determinants of the private investor's decision to enter is done using the probit model, where the dependent variable is a dummy equal to 1 if PPPs were introduced in the relevant segment of the market (respectively in generation, renewable based energy, transmission and distribution, transmission, distribution) and 0 if not (see table C.1).

Table C.1 List of Dependent Variables

Variables	Definition
1. PPP introduction (probit) **Generation**	
Introduction of PPP in GEN	= 1 since the year of establishment of the first PPP in generation = 0 otherwise
Introduction of PPPs in RE	= 1 since the year of establishment of the first PPP in renewables = 0 otherwise
Introduction of PPPs in FF	= 1 since the year of establishment of the first PPP in fossil fuels = 0 otherwise
T&D	
Introduction of PPP in T&D	= 1 since the year of establishment of the first PPP in transmission and distribution = 0 otherwise
Introduction of PPP in TRA	= 1 since the year of establishment of the first PPP in transmission = 0 otherwise
Introduction of PPP in DISTR	= 1 since the year of establishment of the first PPP in distribution = 0 otherwise
2. PPP investment (Heckman approach to sample selection) **Generation**	
PPP Investment in GEN	= investment committed by the private sector in electricity generation (US$)
PPP Investment in RE	= investment committed by the private sector in renewable-based generation (US$)
PPP Investment in FF	= investment committed by the private sector in fossil fuel-based generation (US$)
T&D	
PPP Investment in T&D	= investment committed by the private sector in transmission and distribution (US$)
PPP Investment in TRA	= investment committed by the private sector in transmission (US$)
PPP Investment in DISTR	= investment committed by the private sector in distribution (US$)

The treatment of the modeling of the key factors affecting the private investor's amount of investment sunk in the sector in the relevant segment of the market (respectively in generation, renewable based energy, transmission and distribution, transmission, distribution) (see the second part of table 2A.1) **is based on Heckman's approach to sample selection.** This distinguishes between (1) the decision on whether to enter the segment of the electricity market (selection equation), and (2) the decision on how much investment to commit to (investment equation).[1] Unlike the Tobit model, the factors that affect the two decisions need not be identical and, where identical, could even be different in the sign of their effect on the decisions. The selection equation relates the choice of whether to attract PPPs (via a zero/one dummy variable) as a function of the governance variables and the price of oil is estimated over the complete set of countries using a probit model. The second-stage equation, relating PPP investment to the full set of short-run and long-run variables described in table C.2, is estimated over the sub-set of countries. Because the

Table C.2 Explanatory Variables Influencing PPP in the Power Sector (Expected Relationship)

Variables	Definition	Exp. Sign		
		GEN	*RE*	*T&D*
Sectoral governance variables				
Introduction of feed-in tariffs *FIT*	= 1 since the year of establishment of a feed-in tariff system = 0 otherwise	+	+	—
Introduction of a regulatory agency *REG*	= 1 since the year of establishment of a regulatory agency = 0 otherwise	+	+	+
Sequencing of policy (introduction of private sector first in distribution)	= 1 when PPPs have been introduced first in distribution and then in generation = 0 otherwise	—	—	+
Economy-wide governance variables				
Control of corruption	= measures the perceptions of the extent to which public power is exercised for private gain, including both petty and grand forms of corruption, as well as "capture" of the state by elites and private interests. (Kaufmann and Kray World Governance Indicator)	+	+	+
Degree of democracy *Polity2*	= Revised Combined Polity Score (Polity 2): This variable is a modified version of the POLITY variable to facilitate the use of the POLITY regime measure in time-series analyses. It ranges from +10 (strongly democratic) to –10 (strongly autocratic), based on 6 indicators.	+	+	+
Long-run environmental sustainability factors				
Price of oil	= value of the international price of oil	?	—	—
Kyoto protocol	= 1 for the years after 2005 = 0 otherwise	+	+	—
PPP transmission investment	= investment in transmission committed by the private sector in (US$)	—	+	—
PPP investment in renewables	= committed investment in renewables (US$ million)	—	—	+

(table continues on next page)

Table C.2 Explanatory Variables Influencing PPP in the Power Sector (Expected Relationship) *(continued)*

Variables	Definition	Exp. Sign GEN	RE	T&D
Long-run economic fundamentals				
GDP *ln_GDP*	= GDP, PPP terms (constant 2005 international US$)	+	+	+
Population *ln_Pop*	= total population	+	+	+

Note: ⸺ = variable not included in the regression.

group has been selected by the first-stage equation, the possibility of selection bias would be introduced if a standard regression were used at the second stage. This bias is related to the magnitude of the correlation between the errors (that include the omitted variables) in the selection and investment equations. Where there is no correlation between these errors, there is no selection bias. The direction of the bias depends on the sign of the inter-equation error correlation.

The condition for identification of the Heckman estimation procedure is that the selection equation contains a significant variable(s) not included in the investment equation. The significance of the Mills' ratio in the second stage indicates whether there would have been selection bias in its absence. If the Mills' ratio is insignificant, a simple regression of the quantity of investment on explanatory variables would be unbiased. The canonical Heckman model also assumes that the errors are jointly normal. If that assumption fails, the estimator is generally inconsistent and can provide misleading inference in small samples.

Note

1. The data on the dependent variable consist of observations related to the investment. This would be zero for countries that had not attracted PPPs, and positive for those countries that had decided to use it. This observation is split into two components: a zero or one variable indicating the lack of entry or entry of PPPs, and a variable measuring investment for the subset of countries that attracted PPPs.